SELECTED CLIMBS
IN THE
DESERT
SOUTHWEST

COLORADO
& UTAH

SELECTED CLIMBS IN THE DESERT SOUTHWEST

COLORADO & UTAH

CAMERON M. BURNS

THE
MOUNTAINEERS

To Eric Bjørnstad, a truly remarkable scholar,
climber, and human being, and his Australian shepherd, Rilke

Published by
The Mountaineers
1001 SW Klickitat Way, Suite 201
Seattle, WA 98134

First edition, 1999

Published simultaneously in Great Britain by Cordee, 3a DeMontfort Street, Leicester, England, LE1 7HD

Manufactured in Canada

Edited by Kris Fulsaas
Maps by Gray Mouse Graphics
Cover and book design by Jennifer LaRock Shontz
Layout by Gray Mouse Graphics

Cover photographs: Front: *Jesse Harvey on pitch 4, Stolen Chimney, Ancient Art, Fisher Towers, Utah* © Cameron M. Burns Back: *Jon Butler jumaring on Space Shot, Zion National Park, Utah* © Cameron M. Burns
Frontispiece: *Jon Butler on pitch 3, North Face Standard Route, Castleton Tower.* Photo by Luke Laeser/Butler collection.

Library of Congress Cataloging-in-Publication Data
Burns, Cameron M.
    Selected climbs in the desert southwest / Cameron M. Burns.
    p.   cm.
    Includes bibliographical references and index.
    ISBN 0-89886-657-X (pbk.)
    1. Mountaineering—Southwest, New Guidebooks. 2. Southwest, New Guidebooks. I. Title.
    GV199.42.S68 B87 1999
    796.52'2'0979—dc21
                                                    99-6579
                                                    CIP

CONTENTS

SOUTHWESTERN UTAH

ACKNOWLEDGMENTS

Many people helped on this guidebook by providing information on unknown new routes, as well as descriptions and photos of long-standing classics, and examined my notes carefully. These prolific desert climbers include Mike Baker, Steve Bartlett, Jon Butler, John Catto, Paul Gagner, James "10-4" Garrett, Luke Laeser, John Middendorf, Mike Pennings, Duane Raleigh, Drew Spaulding, Ed Webster, and, last but not least, Jeff Widen.

Also, thanks to others whose company I've enjoyed during nearly two decades of desert climbing: Benny Bach, Fred Beckey, Curtis Benally, Marty Benally, Jeff Bowman, Chuck and Suzanne Brown, Lefty Angus Burns, Jordan Campbell, Jumar Joe Coll, Erik Cook, Steven Dean, Pete Doorish, Ben Dover, Chris Ducker, Jimmy Dunn, Chris Eng, Paul Fehlau, I. P. Freely, Charlie "FBI" French, Bryan Gall, Pat Goodman, Wilson Goodrich, Aaron Gulley, Jesse "The Body" Harvey, David Hayes, Leslie Henderson, Brent Higgins, Warren Hollinger, Mike Hunt, Dan Langmade, Dave Littman, Phil MacCracken, Dougald MacDonald, Mel MacDonnel, Charles Martin, Stan Mish, Jodie "F.C." Murdoch, Andrew Nichols, Linus Platt, Steve Porcella, Ethan Putterman, Keith Reynolds, Glen Rink, Mike Schillaci, Slim Shady, Jeff Singer, Brian Takei, Mark Van Dome, and, last but not least, the Old Ball and Chain (a.k.a. my beautiful wife), Ann Burns.

Eric Bjørnstad was generous with his humungous files of historical information—portions of which I created myself, sent to Eric, then lost at home—and has always let me warm up in his Moab home when things got nasty out. Thanks, Eric.

The highly talented and wonderful Kris Fulsaas was my editor and without her incredible interpretation skills, this ream of pages could not be read by English-speaking peoples. It would be a collection of Cro-Magnonesque grunts and body gestures.

Also thanks to Tommy Myers, Nick Yardley, Steve Srednick, Dawn Widen, Pete Athans, Charlie Fowler, Brian Long, Patrick Kelly, Dale Bard, Dean Cummings, Sylvia and Bob Robertson, Mary and Kerry Burns, Mike Smith, and Valerie Ng.

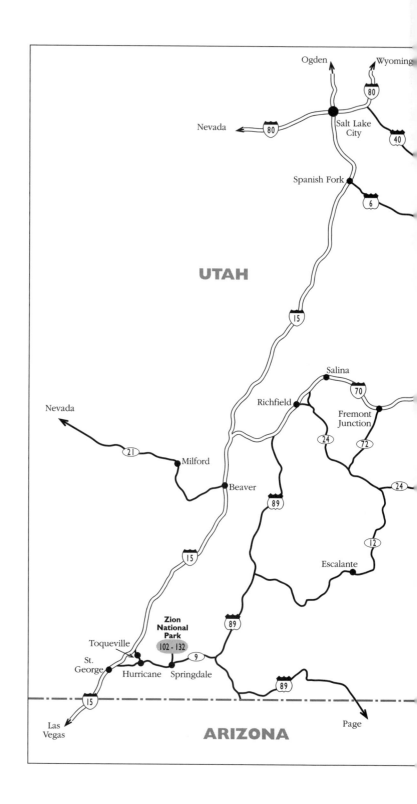

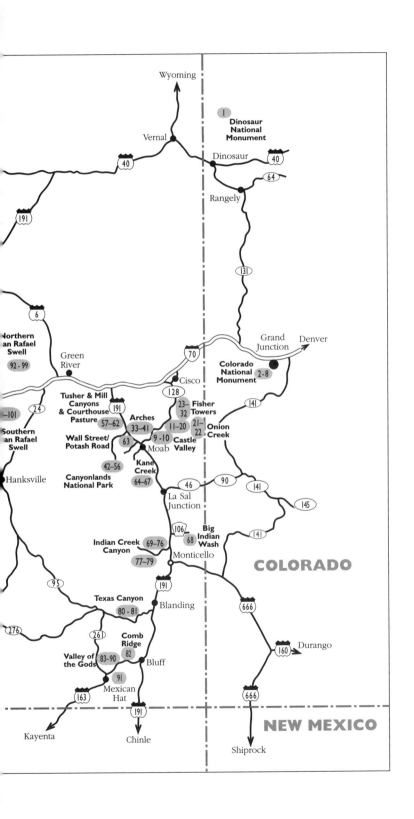

INTRODUCTION

The desert country of the Colorado Plateau is some of the most strikingly beautiful country in the world. Tall sandstone spires and mesas jut skyward into a stark blue sky, and narrow canyons of red rock and sand contrast easily with lush Mormon tea and bright green juniper bushes. Cold winter snowstorms are often followed by intense spring heat waves. Powerful, muddy rivers plow through areas receiving barely a few inches of rain a year.

Without question, the desert country of the southwestern United States is a land of surprise and awe. It's no wonder the region has drawn the attention of philosophers, writers, artists, adventurers, and scholars for more than 100 years.

The region is also one of the finest areas on the planet for rock climbing. Because America's desert southwest is blessed with reasonable temperatures most of the year and very little precipitation, it is possible to climb throughout it every month of the year. And contrary to the myth heard by some who have never visited the southwest desert regions for climbing, the rock is, for the most part, pretty good.

Likewise, the desert has a fascinating climbing history. Some of the best-known characters in all of North American mountaineering have left their respective marks on desert climbing, and to climb routes first ascended by these daring pioneers makes one realize the boldness of these early visitors.

The stories of Layton Kor and his partners forging their way up the Titan, Standing Rock, Monster Tower, and other fabulous desert spires are the stuff of legend. Harvey T. Carter's painstaking efforts to climb every tower in the Fisher Towers, is—to those who have climbed in the Fishers—almost beyond comprehension. And Jimmy Dunn's twenty-five-year pursuit of hard free-climbing in the region—though barely recorded—is without parallel.

On top of all this, the desert is so incredibly beautiful, so wonderously different from most places on the planet, that even if you don't get to climb every day of your trip there, you'll still have a remarkable time. As Chuck Pratt noted in his historic piece, "The View From Deadhorse Point": "To gain any lasting worth from what the desert has to offer, we had to learn to put our pitons and ropes away and to go exploring in silence, keeping our eyes very open. It wasn't easy. We wasted a lot of time climbing until we got the knack."

So, you might well ask, why another guidebook to climbing among the beautiful sandstone canyons and mesas of the desert Southwest? Certainly, desert pioneer and historian Eric Bjørnstad has covered these regions exceptionally well in a series of comprehensive guides that began coming out in 1988.

There are several reasons. One, over the past few years, as friends from Europe

Ed Webster on pitch 2, Honeymoon Chimney, The Priest. Photo by Patrick Griffin/Ed Webster collection.

and Australia have visited and I've loaded them down with two or three of Bjørnstad's guidebooks at a time, plus others, and earmarked the pages with great routes, I came to realize that just one book covering a sampling of the desert's absolute finest areas, routes, spires, and walls is desperately needed. This guide will never replace Bjørnstad's superhuman efforts to chronicle all canyon-country climbing, but it does sort out the wheat from the chaff, and will become a valuable tool for those with limited time and those seeking to climb the most classic routes in the desert. In short, this guidebook is an appetite-whetting sampler of the best the desert has to offer. Do even a handful of the routes described in this guidebook, and you'll be hooked on desert rock forever.

CLIMBING IN THE DESERT

If you're a rock climber, climbing in the desert is probably the most demanding type of climbing you will ever try. The rock can be horrendous in places. The anchors can be, sometimes, frightening. And it's not rare to find a 3-pitch tower more psychologically difficult than a 10-pitch route on granite or gneiss.

Climbing in the desert is serious business. You need to know your rock craft inside and out. Big-wall techniques are helpful, even on the shortest routes. You need to examine anchors left by previous parties and judge for yourself whether they are still intact enough for you to use, or whether you should add a new sling or even a new anchor. You need to know whether you have the wherewithal to pull off a route. Sometimes you won't, and that's okay. Come back later. These routes aren't the Bastille Crack or Nutcracker. Every single desert route you get on demands a healthy shot of respect.

Many of the bigger routes described in this guidebook are very committing and experience-demanding climbs. If you're a desert neophyte, to think that you can go from an ascent of the Kor-Ingalls route on Castleton Tower one day to an ascent of the Finger of Fate route on the Titan the next day might get you into more trouble (and embarrassment) than you can imagine. The point of this guidebook is not to instruct you in climbing techniques or desert climbing techniques (see the Annotated Bibliography for some suggestions), but to show you where these climbs are and how good they can be. I strongly recommend that you climb *a lot* before you visit the desert, and build up slowly to doing the bigger routes. That way, you can gain valuable experience and still, hopefully, have fun.

Weather (i.e., rain) in the desert can be a big concern. Sandstone is highly porous compared to all other rock types, and wet sandstone can be dangerous. Most people coming to the canyon country of the southwest have already heard stories of Zion's rock losing two-thirds to three-quarters of its holding power when it's soaked. The same can be true of other types of sandstone (especially Cutler and Entrada). The best advice is to avoid climbing when it's raining, and let the rock dry out (at least a day, oftentimes longer) before beginning any route. There is no hard and fast rule about when you can safely begin a climb after a big storm, but use common sense and a cautious attitude whenever you consider starting up a sandstone climb.

Other things to be aware of when climbing in the desert are the same rules that apply for all climbing areas: Carry adequate water and food; bring sunscreen and first-aid materials; wear appropriate clothing; and don't forget your helmet.

CLEAN CLIMBING

"Clean climbing" is a term that refers to the use of equipment that doesn't permanently scar or alter the rock. In most climbing areas, clean climbing is practiced through the use of gear such as wired stoppers or nuts, camming devices, and anything that wedges or cams.

In recent years, there has been a huge trend in the desert toward "clean" climbing. Unfortunately, the debate has many complex facets and subtle nuances that inexperienced desert climbers might not fully comprehend. Here are a few personal observations:

First, in some situations, poorly done "clean" climbing can do as much damage to the rock as the use of pitons. (Note that I say "can.") A climber yanking out a totally crunched-in camming unit can do as much damage as an experienced nailer gently tapping out a Birdbeak, often more. Stoppers can be even worse; poor technique in yanking out stoppers that have been weighted can be incredibly damaging. The Touchstone Wall in Zion National Park, for example, is slowly being erased because of poorly retrieved stoppers.

Second, although doing routes clean is what we should aspire to, the reality is that often it's not possible for everyone. Some of those talented climbers doing first clean ascents are not only outstanding clean direct-aid climbers, but they are also incredibly talented free-climbers, and in some cases have free-climbed through short sections of aid that most mortals probably could not free-climb.

Third, nearly all the routes in this guidebook (free and clean included) rely on fixed gear, which oftentimes means pre-fixed pitons. Though these pitons might have been in place during the first or subsequent clean ascent, there's no guarantee they'll remain. Hence, repeating a route that has been done clean and had its fixed pins removed can be almost impossible or at least difficult.

Fourth, even if a route has been done "clean," there's no guarantee that every ascent party *can* do it clean. That's because on some routes the rock can be so soft that even a well-placed camming unit or (more commonly) stopper can break out portions of a placement long after the first clean ascent. I remember tugging gently down on a couple of stopper placements on routes in the Fishers, only to see an entire placement crumble away. (This is a rare situation, but worth noting.)

Finally, "clean" is a relative term that maybe everyone needs to ponder a little bit more thoroughly. With even the best, most carefully placed equipment, a grain or two of sand will likely get rubbed or knocked off. Even the most talented climber will drag his or her body, ropes, and bags across the surface of the stone, causing some wear. Despite all the hoopla surrounding the concept of clean, it might be a weird, distorted myth.

Still, after all those points, the use of wired stoppers and camming units should, hopefully, limit the wear and tear on most routes included in this guidebook. Before you visit the desert, be well versed in the intricacies of stopper and camming unit

Cam Burns falling off the traverse on pitch 2, Kor Route, Standing Rock, Canyonlands National Park. Photo: Jon Butler/Burns collection.

use. And be especially careful when you remove gear. Then use clean gear whenever you can—and even when you think you can't. You'll be proud, your mom will be proud of you, and you'll have friends in the parking lot when you're done.

A WORD ABOUT DESCENTS

Descents are always the most important aspect of a climb. Often the desert, like the high mountains, does not provide you with a straightforward rappel or scramble back to terra firma. Descents are often the trickiest part of a desert route. Ropes can get hung up on weird gargoyles (as in the Fisher Towers) or snagged on calcite flakes (common in Castle Valley). Anchors can be suspect at best, and lines of descent can deviate from the climbing route in weird and scary ways.

Zion National Park probably has the most intricate descents of any climbing area in the country. Here, rappel routes meander casually through wooded slopes only to drop off of 1,000-foot precipices via slings tied around trees and hard-to-find rock anchors. With many parties topping out on Zion routes after dark, it is especially important that these descents be respected as far more committing than any ascent! Of course, you know what to do: Be careful; take headlamps, a bolt kit, and slings just in case; be prepared to sit out the night if you have to; and be experienced enough to get yourself out of trouble should it arise.

FIXED ANCHORS IN THE DESERT

Simply stated, fixed anchors in the desert can be horrible. And they can be even worse than that.

Just before this guidebook went to press, I went out to the Fisher Towers to check out the Hippie Route on Ancient Art, as Duane Raleigh had told me it was good (for the Fishers). It was. My partner, Bryan Gall, scratched around in the summit and, to our surprise, found an old fixed pin. He clipped it, then lowered off, only to have it pop after 5 feet of lowering. Bryan zinged past me headfirst into the chimney below. The pin, which was merely an inch long, had probably been there since the first ascent and was about as solid as an ocean yacht made of typing paper. A few weeks later, Mike Baker described to me his pulling a pin off the North Face (a.k.a. Regular Route) on River Tower. Same short, worthless pins (short knifeblades with rings) everyone's been aiding up—as if they were ⅜-inch bolts in granite—forever.

I've been fortunate in that I've never had fixed gear in the desert rip on me, but that doesn't mean that everyone who uses this guidebook will want to trust it. Check it out. Sniff it. If it doesn't smell right, don't use it. Back it up with something off your rack, and never let anyone give you a hard time about beefing up an anchor or replacing one that's old. The Fisher Towers' fixed anchors are probably the worst you'll encounter anywhere, and the fact that some of them are now four decades old means they should be treated with great care.

The term "bolt" in this guidebook refers not only to the standard types of bolts found throughout the world (devices that are held in place by metal collars or parts that expand by being screwed tight) but also to "drilled angles." Drilled angles—which were perfected by Harvey Carter in the early 1950s for climbing at Garden of

Jeff Singer on pitch 4, Stuffin' Nuts, Chip Tower, Canyonlands National Park. © Jeff Widen.

the Gods—are simply angle pitons (usually ½ inch or ⅝ inch) that have been smashed into ⅜-inch holes. The quality of the rock generally dictates the size of piton that gets placed in the hole. Some climbers consider drilled angles the best form of anchor in the desert (which is debatable) but, as with other anchors, they occasionally need replacing. On some routes one might find Lost Arrows, and even ¾-inch angle pitons smashed into holes. The Lost Arrows are sometimes simply a matter of the first-ascent party running out of ½-inch and ⅝-inch angles, while a ¾-inch angle usually means the rock is so soft that smaller angles would not have been secure. Regardless, this book refers to all of these fixed anchors as "bolts."

HOW TO USE THIS BOOK

This guidebook is arranged in an east-to-west fashion, starting with desert routes in western Colorado and moving west, across the Colorado Plateau to southwestern Utah. Although certain areas have been omitted (like Red Rocks in southern Nevada and the areas around Sedona, Arizona), the "desert" to many climbers means southeastern Utah, hence the majority of the routes in this guidebook are in southeastern Utah. However, a few remote climbs are also included, either because they offer great climbing or are historically important (the Kor Route on Steamboat Rock, for example), or both. At least if you travel to some of these remote routes, you will have the opportunity to see new areas and experience parts of the desert you might not otherwise see.

Each chapter introduction includes information on **area climbing regulations, special considerations,** and driving directions (**getting there**). From where you park your vehicle, follow the **approach** (given for each route) to reach the starting point of the climb.

Routes, Ratings, and Racks

Each of the routes described is numbered on the overview map, showing the route's general location. There are written descriptions for each route, along with either a photo or a topographic diagram of the route, sometimes both. This information, combined with your own experience and knowledge, will get you to the climbs and up them safely. Each route includes information on **first ascent, difficulty** rating, **time** required for the climb, recommended **equipment, approach, route** description, and **descent.**

Under **difficulty** are several ratings, including the route's grade (in roman numerals); the free-climbing difficulty (which runs from Class 1 through Class 5); a direct aid rating with either an "A" prefix or a "C" prefix; and, occasionally, a rating used to describe difficult-to-protect pitches (R).

Grades (I through VI) describe the length of time required for a route and its overall commitment level, and are broken down thus:

Grade I: 1–3 hours
Grade II: 3–4 hours
Grade III: 4–6 hours
Grade IV: 1 full day
Grade V: 1–2 days, usually involving a bivouac
Grade VI: 3 days or more

Free-climbing ratings are divided into "Classes," thus:
Class 1: Walking on level ground
Class 2: Hiking on rough terrain
Class 3: Hiking over rough ground where the hands must be used for balance
Class 4: Scrambling on rough, steep terrain that is exposed; many climbers
 will want a rope on Class 4 terrain
Class 5: Climbing, in which a rope and protection are generally necessary for
 upward progress (Class 5 climbing is further broken down into decimal
 ratings, from 5.0 to 5.14)

Direct aid climbing (also known as Class 6 climbing) has ratings broken down into six categories, from A0 to A5. In clean aid climbing ratings, the prefix "A" is replaced by a "C," to indicate that the route has been done without hammers. Ratings are considered thus:

A0/C0: A "rest point" in which the climber uses gear to hold his or her
 weight; no upward progress is made
A1/C1: A bomber placement that is unlikely to be pulled out in the event of a fall
A2/C2: Fairly good placement that will hold a moderate fall

A3/C3: A placement that will hold body weight, but is unlikely to hold anything more than a short fall

A4/C4: Very difficult aid in which many A3 placements are strung together; all the placements will pull in the event of a fall

A5/C5: Extremely tenuous gear placements that somehow manage to hold body weight; "start praying" territory

Finally, many climbers use a rating to describe the availability of protection on a route. One of these rating systems (there are several) rates routes using the same letters that Hollywood filmmakers use to rate movies: G, R, and X. In climbing, these ratings mean the following:

G: (for general audiences) Protection is excellent

R: (for mature audiences) Protection is difficult and you might take a long fall, resulting in injury

X: (for serious adults only) Protection is nonexistent and you might die if you fall

Traditionally, climbs with G protection ratings have the "G" dropped from their description. (A route rated III, 5.8, therefore, would have excellent protection.) Only routes with sparse protection

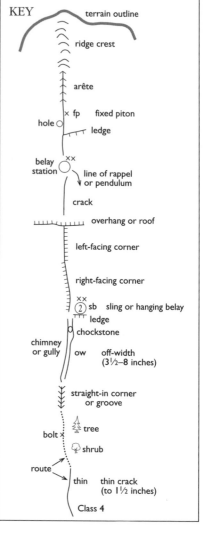

("R" and "X" routes) are generally labeled with these esoteric distinctions. This guidebook contains no X-rated climbs, but occasionally you will encounter routes that have "R" added to their rating. If you lead one of these R-rated pitches, you should be very solid on terrain of that difficulty.

Desert ratings can be funky. A 5.10 hand crack can be harder or easier if your hands are big or small. Face-climbing can get sandy, and a pitch of 5.9 friction can often feel much harder, depending on how clean or dirty the route is on that particular day.

In twenty years of climbing, I have never, ever seen equipment information match what I needed on a climb. Even on routes I've put up, I've found that other parties repeated the climb with totally different gear from what I used.

Hence, route equipment in this guide is given as a recommendation, not an absolute. Often, rack information was provided by first-ascent parties and/or subsequent ascent parties, and can differ wildly from what you might or might not find necessary. I have attempted to get consensus from at least a few climbers who have done the route and to list what most climbers use on a particular route. However, it is imperative that you—the one doing the actual climbing—judge for yourself, to the best of your ability, what you'll need. Go up to the base of the route and sniff around. Consider what you'll likely need before you start climbing. The gear recommendations don't include the obvious things like carabiners and slings; those should be taken for granted.

The time estimates given in this book—with the exception of routes in Zion National Park—include the time it takes to hike to and from the route (from a vehicle), as well as the time it takes to climb the route. Because of the unique nature of most Zion routes, the time estimates given for them are only for the ascent portion of a climb. Humping loads to the bases of routes can take some parties a full day, as can descents. It is important that Zion climbers make their own time estimates based on their experience and skill. Remember, times given in this book are only estimates.

Area Land Regulations

Many of these routes lie in national parks, and it is becoming increasingly important that climbers check the current status of routes at the park visitor center before beginning a climb.

Many areas of the desert are seeing an increase in awareness about nesting raptors. In recent years, formations in various parks that, ten years ago, might not have been affected have seen closures. (This is probably due to an increase in human awareness about raptors, rather than an increase in raptor populations.)

Rock formation closures are especially significant in Zion National Park, where entire sections of the canyon can be closed.

For more information, call the park numbers listed below.

Arches National Park: 435-259-8161
Canyonlands National Park: 435-259-7164
Colorado National Monument: 970-858-3617
Dinosaur National Monument: 970-374-3017
Zion National Park: 435-772-0170

About the Routes Selected

In the early 1990s, I had a list in my head of the most classic desert routes and figured they would one day make it into some kind of guidebook. As the decade passed, Eric Bjørnstad released his *Desert Rock: Rock Climbs in the National Parks,* which includes a selection of Zion wall routes recommended by John Middendorf, and Stewart Green put out his *Rock Climbing Utah,* which used Bjørnstad's copious notes as a basis. However, I began to see that many newer routes, as well as some obscure classics, have never made it into previously published guidebooks and needed to be included in this volume.

That's why you'll find in this book classic routes that are virtually unknown (like Gentleman's Agreement in Zion, for example), alongside classics that have been written about ad nauseum (Touchstone Wall in Zion, for example). Both are great routes, but the inclusion of forgotten classics like Gentleman's Agreement is one of the highlights of this book. (Ironically, Zion's most popular summer route, the north face of Ashtar Command, has never been published anywhere.)

Also, in many areas you might show up to do a classic route, only to be thwarted by long lines of waiting climbers. Hence, in most cases where I describe a classic route, I've tried to add another nearby route as an alternative.

The climbs found in this guidebook cover a wide range of desert climbing experiences. From easy free-climbs to difficult aid routes, each one of the routes has been selected for the quality of the climbing, the setting in which it is found, and the formation on which it is located. Not everyone using this book will think of the Fisher Towers' Titan's Finger of Fate route as high-quality, fun climbing, but the formation itself and the history of the route make it very classic indeed.

Speaking of the Fisher Towers, some climbers might argue that there's not a single route in the Fishers that warrants "classic" status. They're dirty, rotten affairs at best, and can be absolute nightmares under certain situations. But for sandstone aficionados, the Fisher Towers area boasts its own remarkable charm. What is important about these routes is that you consider them within their own context. It's impossible to compare routes in Indian Creek Canyon with routes in, say, Arches National Park. They are different areas with different rock types and different challenges, sometimes requiring different climbing techniques.

Admittedly, most of the routes in this guidebook are located on towers, because desert summits are wonderful places and the kinds of climbs that make the desert unique. But there are some "wall"-type routes included as well (almost all the Zion National Park routes are walls). Hopefully the mixture will keep you entertained for a few seasons.

ENVIRONMENTAL CONSIDERATIONS

Environmental considerations are the single most important aspect of any route you do in the desert. Everything about the desert, from the soil and plant life to the very rock you climb on, is far more fragile than in any other climbing area on the North American continent. Thus it is imperative that you follow some basic guidelines to avoid impacting the area.

First, do not drive where roads don't exist. There are plenty of dirt roads criss-crossing even the remotest parts of the desert, so making your own is both selfish and incredibly damaging to the fragile desert soils.

Second, avoid creating new trails to the base of routes. Stay on existing trails. The cryptobiotic soil that is common throughout the desert southwest is a living, growing entity, and it takes the soil centuries to recover from only one person walking across it. If a trail to a tower or route is not immediately obvious, look around. You'll find it with a little bit of searching.

Third, human waste is starting to be an issue in certain areas. If nature calls, make sure you are at least 300 feet from any watercourses. (Remember, watercourses can often be dry.) Bury human excrement at least 8 inches in the soil, and pack out any toilet paper. The same rules apply around the bases of the most popular routes. Go some distance from the climb—at least 300 feet—before you conduct your business.

Fourth, use climbing equipment that doesn't create a visual impact. Besides using "clean climbing" techniques wherever possible (see above), also use brown or red chalk and brown or black anchor slings.

Fifth, avoid archaeological sites. To the best of my knowledge, there are no documented Native American ruins near any of the routes in this guidebook, but that doesn't mean that they might not be there. If you see anything looking remotely like a stone wall, a pot sherd, or another Native American artifact, leave it alone—stealing Native American artifacts is a serious crime, and you could wind up with not only jail time, but a hefty fine. Most important of all, if you spot an artifact, do not tell anyone about it.

—Cameron M. Burns

A NOTE ABOUT SAFETY

Safety is an important concern in all outdoor activities. No guidebook can alert you to every hazard or anticipate the limitations of every reader. Therefore, the descriptions of roads, trails, routes, and natural features in this book are not representations that a particular place or excursion will be safe for your party. When you follow any of the routes described in this book, you assume responsibility for your own safety. Under normal conditions, such excursions require the usual attention to traffic, road and trail conditions, weather, terrain, the capabilities of your party, and other factors. Keeping informed on current conditions and exercising common sense are the keys to a safe, enjoyable outing.

—The Mountaineers

DINOSAUR NATIONAL MONUMENT

Dinosaur National Monument is a spectacular place, with towering, 1,000-foot sandstone walls and huge warped canyons that were one result of the uplifting of the Rocky Mountains.

The park is best known for its massive concentration of dinosaur fossils, which were first discovered in 1908 by Earl Douglass of the Carnegie Museum in Pittsburg. In 1915, after Douglass and his men had been extracting fossils for about six years from an area that is now the western edge of the park, the quarry was designated a national monument. In 1938, the park was expanded to include the canyons of the Green and Yampa Rivers. In the early 1950s, the federal government began considering a dam in Dinosaur National Monument, a concept many of the era's leading environmentalists fought against, including David Brower. The dam was never built.

In 1965, Layton Kor, Michael Covington, and Brian Marts traveled to the monument to make the first ascent of Steamboat Rock, via its east face.

Area climbing regulations: At present, Dinosaur National Monument has no climbing regulations of its own, but regulations common to all national parks and monuments apply. The most important of these regulations include the prohibition of electric drills and the encouragement of clean climbing.

Special considerations: The trip into Echo Park takes a traveler many miles over rough roads. It is best to call monument officials (970-374-2450) to check Echo Park Road's condition before traveling all the way to northwestern Colorado. Once you reach Echo Park, some kind of boat, canoe, or raft is needed to get across the river to the route.

Getting there: To reach Dinosaur National Monument and Steamboat Rock, drive east from the town of Dinosaur, Colorado, on US 40 for 2 miles to the entrance to the monument. Turn left onto the Monument Road.

Follow this road for about 27.4 miles, crossing into Utah and then back into Colorado. At 27.4 miles, turn right, onto the Echo Park Road. Follow the Echo Park Road for about 8.2 miles, to a T intersection. At this intersection, turn left and follow Moffat County Road 156 for 4.2 miles to Echo Park. Steamboat Rock is obvious to the north, across the river. Turn right, and drive northeast along the river's edge for about 0.3 mile to a small parking area. Park here. The route is obvious across the river from the parking lot.

James Garrett leading above the Eagle's Nest Alcove on the Kor Route, Steamboat Rock, Dinosaur National Monument. Photo by Mark Synnott/Garrett collection.

1 STEAMBOAT ROCK, KOR ROUTE (A.K.A. KOR-COVINGTON-MARTS ROUTE)

First ascent: Layton Kor, Michael Covington, and Brian Marts, 1965
Difficulty: IV, 5.10, A2
Time: 2 days
Equipment: 2 sets of Friends or Camalots; 2 sets of TCUs; a piton rack with knifeblades, Leeper Z's, Lost Arrows, and small angles; Camalots to #4
Approach: Once you reach Echo Park, cross the river in a boat, canoe, or raft to get to the wall.

Route: Pitch 1: Start nailing and nutting up a right-facing dihedral past some bolts to a small roof, surmount the roof (A2), and reach a 2- to 3-inch crack. Belay at the bolts or at the wider section of the crack above. Pitch 2: Continue straight up the widening crack, via either free-climbing (5.10) or easy aid-climbing (A1). Pitch 3: Follow the crack (5.10 or C1) to the very prominent ledge (the Eagle's Nest Alcove), where the remnants of the abandoned nest still grace the ledge, and a two-bolt belay. Pitch 4: Nail (A2+) out the impressive Cave Roof Pitch above the Eagle's Nest Alcove to a belay ledge above. Pitch 5: Continue up the same crack system through some smaller roofs and increasingly easier terrain to a belay (5.10, A1). Pitch 6: Climb the 5.10+ crack above as it gets progressively easier, then Class 4 to the top of the mesa.

Special considerations: In 1993, there was a hornets' nest at the top of pitch 1. Though the nest is gone now, the hornets may come back at any time. A can of wasp and hornet insecticide can be handy. Also, this route requires only minimal nailing (on pitches 1 and 4) and will likely go clean in the near future. Most of the pitches are 150–165 feet long.

Descent: From the top and end of the Kor route, walk right or east about 500 feet to a rappel station that descends the north-side slabs. Two ropes and two rappels are needed until one can walk back around to the southeast side.

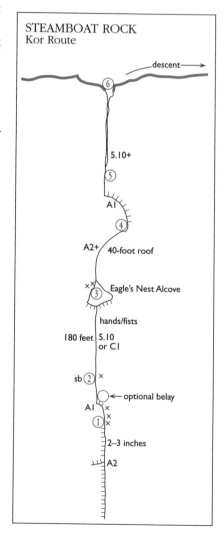

STEAMBOAT ROCK
Kor Route

descent

6

5.10+

5

A1

4

A2+ 40-foot roof

Eagle's Nest Alcove

3

hands/fists

180 feet 5.10 or C1

sb 2

optional belay

A1

1

2–3 inches

A2

COLORADO NATIONAL MONUMENT

Colorado National Monument is a wonderful chunk of desert country sliced off from Utah and hard up against the western edge of the Mile High State. Located just southwest of the city of Grand Junction, Colorado, "The Monument," as it's known locally, features many networks of unique canyons sitting on the northern edge of a large mesa. Not only do the canyons feature excellent climbing opportunities, but the position and location of The Monument mean that although you are climbing in a wilderness setting, you look down upon a very urban environment (Grand Junction) in the valley below. This situation can't but help remind one of why many of us climb to begin with: to escape the human world. In The Monument, there are numerous routes for escape.

Area climbing regulations: Climbers should check at the visitor center for the current status of climbing in the park. Certain formations can be closed for nesting raptors. In recent years, Independence Monument (climb 4) has seen some closures for nesting peregrine falcons. Colorado National Monument does allow the use of pitons and the placement of bolts; however the park service asks climbers not to place fixed gear unless an existing anchor is deemed unsafe. Motorized drills and non-brown webbing are prohibited.

Special considerations: Although the rock in The Monument is technically Wingate sandstone, the hardest of all the desert sandstones, it's a type of Wingate that is much softer than the Wingate found in Indian Creek Canyon and Castle Valley. Monument Wingate is much more like Entrada sandstone, and should be treated with both respect and caution.

Getting to the West Entrance area: To reach Colorado National Monument's West Entrance, take the Fruita exit (exit 19) off I-70, west of Grand Junction, Colorado, and drive east on Hwy. 340 for about 2.5 miles. Turn right onto Rim Rock Drive (unmarked) and pass the West Entrance station to The Monument. From the West Entrance station, drive 1.8 miles to a small pullout on the right side of the road, just uphill from the Balanced Rock pullout. The Ribbed Buttress Route (climb 2) takes a prominent crack system on the wall above the road. At 4.2 miles past the West Entrance station is the visitor center area. To reach Sentinel Spire (climb 3), turn left onto the unnamed road just before the visitor center (this road leads to the amphitheater/picnic area/campground complex) and follow it straight (don't turn left into the campground) for about 0.3 mile, until it becomes a one-way road and a left-hand turn into a large parking lot must be made. To reach Grandview Spire (climb 5) and the Kissing Couple (a.k.a. Bell Tower, climb 6), drive 6 miles past the West Entrance station to the Grand View Overlook. This is a great place to view both spires, especially the Kissing Couple. From the Grand View Overlook, it is possible to drive another 0.5 mile or so and scramble down into the canyon between Grandview Spire and the Kissing Couple to reach their bases. This approach, although short, is very rough and steep. You can also reach these two spires via the Monument Canyon Trail, which is relatively flat most of the way, and most climbers prefer this approach.

Getting to the Monument Canyon Trail: The Monument Canyon Trail provides access to Independence Monument (climb 4), Grandview Spire (climb 5), and

Climb 2, Ribbed Buttress, Ribbed Buttress Route. © Cameron M. Burns.

the Kissing Couple (a.k.a. Bell Tower, climb 6). From the Fruita exit on I-70, drive east on Hwy. 340 about 2.5 miles to the turnoff onto Rim Rock Drive into the West Entrance station. Instead of turning right, into The Monument, continue east on Hwy. 340 for 2.2 miles, then turn right, into a popular small parking area just off the road. This is the trailhead for Monument Canyon Trail.

Getting to the Ute Canyon Trail: To get to Safeway Spire (climb 7) and Oompah Tower (climb 8), from the Fruita exit on I-70 drive east on Hwy. 340 to the turnoff into the West Entrance station. Instead of turning right, into The Monument, continue east on Hwy. 340 for 6.7 miles to the intersection of Redlands Parkway and South Broadway. Turn right, onto South Broadway, and follow it for 1.25 miles to a small suburban street on the right, Wildwood Drive (often the street sign is missing). Follow Wildwood Drive for 0.45 mile as it winds through a small subdivision, then turn right, into the Ute Canyon trailhead parking area.

2   RIBBED BUTTRESS, RIBBED BUTTRESS ROUTE

First ascent: Ron Olevsky, February 1978
Difficulty: III, 5.11, C1 or 5.8, C1
Time: 1 full day
Equipment: 2 sets of camming units with several #4 Camalots; 1 set of wired stoppers
Approach: From the West Entrance station, drive 1.8 miles to a small pullout on the right side of the road, just uphill from the Balanced Rock pullout. The Ribbed Buttress Route takes a prominent crack system on the wall above the road.
Route: Pitch 1: Climb a short corner (5.6) to a 5.7 hand crack that leads to a small ledge and fixed anchors at the base of a large chimney. Pitch 2: Climb the chimney to a hanging belay (5.9). Pitch 3: Climb a right-facing dihedral to a bolt (5.8, C1 or 5.10+), then traverse right, to a hanging belay from fixed anchors. Pitch 4: Traverse right, to the base of a thin crack (C1 or 5.11), which leads to an off-width (5.9) and a small ledge with fixed anchors. Pitch 5: Climb the wide crack above the belay (5.10), which ends at an alcove with a stance. Pitch 6: Move left and climb a bolt ladder (C1) to a ledge. Pitch 7: Climb a left-leaning corner, then a series of ledges and blocks to reach the mesa (5.8).
Special considerations: The route can be done in fewer pitches by linking several together. Also, the route has been almost entirely free-climbed.
Descent: Walk west, across the mesa, to a point where it is possible to down-climb to Rim Rock Drive. It is 0.5 mile or so back along the road east to the pullout.

3   SENTINEL SPIRE, FAST DRAW

First ascents: Layton Kor, Harvey Carter, and John Auld, May 3, 1960. *First solo ascent:* Ron Olevsky, March 1976. *First free ascent:* Andy Petefish and John Christenson, 1978.
Difficulty: II, 5.10
Time: ½ day
Equipment: 2 sets of camming units with extra #1–#3; TCUs; 1 set of wired stoppers

Climb 3, Sentinel Spire, Fast Draw. © Cameron M. Burns.

Approach: From the parking lot (see Getting to the West Entrance area), hike east toward the canyon rim. Sentinel Spire comes into view below the mesa. At this point, it is necessary to rappel into the canyon (leaving a rope fixed for the return journey) and scramble to the base of the north face of the tower, where Fast Draw begins. Start at the bottom of the northwest side of the tower, where there are two obvious cracks.

Route: Pitch 1: Climb up the right crack (5.10-), a perfect hand crack, then face-climb left to the left-hand crack and a fixed belay. Pitch 2: Climb the off-width/chimney above (5.8) to a fixed belay. Pitch 3: Continue up the wide crack above (5.9) to the summit.

Descent: Make two double-rope rappels down the route from fixed anchors.

4 INDEPENDENCE MONUMENT, OTTO'S ROUTE

First ascent: John Otto, June 14, 1911
Difficulty: III, 5.9
Time: 1 full day
Equipment: 1 set of camming units
Approach: Monument Canyon Trail skirts around the back of a subdivision before continuing about 2.5 miles up lower Monument Canyon to the base of Independence Monument, the prominent butte in the middle of the canyon. Start at the bottom of the north side of the tower, below an obvious large, low-angled, left-facing ramp with a crack in the corner.

Route: Pitch 1: Climb the ramp (Class 4/lower Class 5) to a huge, sandy bench. Pitch 2: Climb the wide chimney above and right (5.8) to a small ledge with fixed anchors. Pitch 3: Squeeze through the overhanging slot using drilled pockets (5.8, size dependent). Pitch 4: Walk (Class 1) through the Time Tunnel (a wide slot behind a subsidiary summit of the tower) to a comfortable, spacious ledge, Lunch Box Ledge. Pitch 5: Climb the face above Lunch Box Ledge (5.8), using fixed gear. Pitch 6: The last pitch follows chiseled edges and pockets up the western prow of the tower. The final overhanging moves are protected by pitons hammered into both the rock and the ends of pipes drilled into the rock (5.9).

Special considerations: Since the drilled holes are deteriorating, this route gets a little harder every decade. Old guidebooks call the route 5.8, but many climbers believe it's more like 5.9 and getting harder. Also, since the

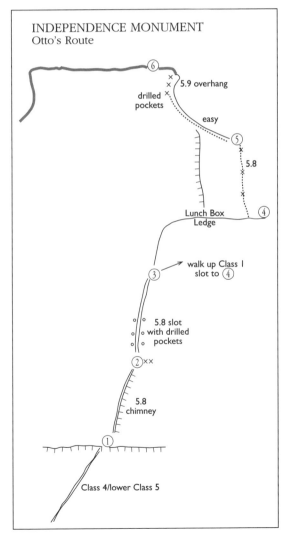

INDEPENDENCE MONUMENT
Otto's Route

Climb 4, Independence Monument, Otto's Route. © Cameron M. Burns.

route is incredibly popular and there still remains much loose rock on the huge ledges, a helmet is a must.

Descent: Make double-rope rappels down the route from fixed anchors.

5   GRANDVIEW SPIRE, RELICS

First ascent: Mike Baker, Bob Wade, and Michael Kennedy, November 13, 1991

Difficulty: IV, 5.10, A2

Time: 1 full day

Equipment: 2 sets of camming units with half sizes; 2 sets TCUs; #5, #6, and #7 Friends; 20 small pitons of various sizes

Approach: There are two ways to reach Grandview Spire. From the Grand View Overlook, it is possible to drive another 0.5 mile or so and scramble down into the canyon between Grandview Spire and the Kissing Couple to reach their bases. This approach, although short, is very rough and steep. You can also take Monument Canyon Trail, which skirts around the back of a subdivision, continues up lower Monument Canyon past Independence Monument, and continues southeast until it passes just below both Grandview Spire and the Kissing Couple. Start at the bottom of the southeast side of the tower, in the same small subsidiary canyon as the hike down to the Kissing Couple from Rim Rock Drive.

Route: Pitch 1: Climb up a splitter hand crack that quickly thins to fingers,

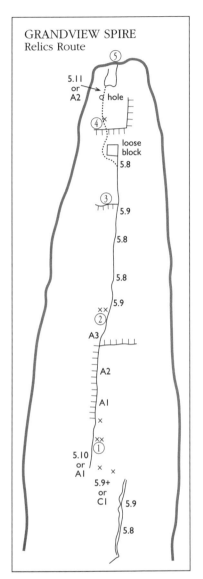

GRANDVIEW SPIRE
Relics Route

⑤
5.11
or
A2   hole
④
loose
block
5.8

③
5.9

5.8

5.8

5.9
××
②
A3

A2

AI
×

××①
5.10
or   ×   ×
AI
5.9+
or
CI   5.9

5.8

Climb 5, Grandview Spire, Relics.
© Cameron M. Burns.

then nothing. Face-climb left (5.9+) past two bolts to a fixed belay in the route's main crack system in a huge right-facing corner (5.10). Pitch 2: Start up the corner, climb a roof, and belay at fixed anchors (A3). Pitch 3: Climb the widening crack above to a ledge (5.9). Pitch 4: Continue up the crack, move left around a large loose block, and belay at the big ledge just below the summit (5.8). Pitch 5: Climb to the top (5.11 or A2).

Special considerations: This route will likely go clean very easily.

Descent: Make double-rope rappels down the original route on the southwest side of the tower.

6 KISSING COUPLE (A.K.A. BELL TOWER), LONG DONG WALL (A.K.A. KOR-CARTER-AULD ROUTE)

First ascents: Layton Kor, Harvey Carter, and John Auld, May 4, 1960. *First solo ascent:* Ron Olevsky, March 1976. *First free ascent:* Andy Petefish and Paul Abbott, 1980.

Difficulty: III, 5.11- or III, 5.10, C1

Time: 1 full day

Equipment: 2 sets of camming units with extra #1–#3; TCUs; 2 sets of wired stoppers

Climb 6, Kissing Couple, Long Dong Wall. © Cameron M. Burns.

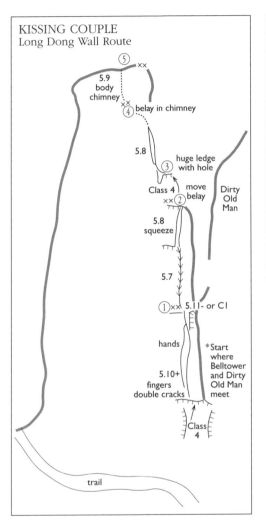

KISSING COUPLE
Long Dong Wall Route

5 — xx
5.9 body chimney
xx belay in chimney
4

5.8
3 huge ledge with hole

Class 4 — move belay
xx 2
Dirty Old Man

5.8 squeeze

5.7

1 xx 5.11- or C1

hands

*Start where Belltower and Dirty Old Man meet

5.10+ fingers double cracks

Class 4

trail

Climb 6, Kissing Couple, Long Dong Wall.
© Cameron M. Burns.

Approach: There are two ways to reach the Kissing Couple. From the Grand View Overlook, drive another 0.5 mile or so and scramble down into the canyon between Grandview Spire and the Kissing Couple to reach their bases. This approach, although short, is very rough and steep. You can also take Monument Canyon Trail, which skirts around the back of a subdivision, continues up lower Monument Canyon past Independence Monument, and continues southeast until it passes just below both Grandview Spire and the Kissing Couple. Start at the bottom of the southwest side of the tower, where the tower meets the canyon wall to the south (called Dirty Old Man). Scramble up a wide slot (Class 4) to the base of an obvious crack system.

Route: Pitch 1: Climb up a thin crack/flake system that gradually widens (5.10+), then step left using a bolt for protection (5.11- or C1) to a belay. Pitch 2: Climb the gully above (5.7) for 50 feet, then squeeze up the unprotected 5.8 chimney above to a belay. Pitch 3: Scramble right and up 40 feet to a short chimney, then squeeze through a crack to a big sort of sunken ledge and a belay. Pitch 4: Climb the obvious 5.8 hand crack/stemming corner and follow it up to a belay inside the tower. Pitch 5: A wide body stem past several pieces of fixed gear (5.9) leads to the summit.

Descent: Make a double-rope rappel from the summit to the top of pitch 3. Then rappel the route.

7 SAFEWAY SPIRE, FIVE FINGER DISCOUNT
First ascent: Jon Butler and Cameron Burns, April 8, 1995 (Luke Laeser worked on the first pitch)
Difficulty: IV, 5.10+, A1
Time: 1 full day

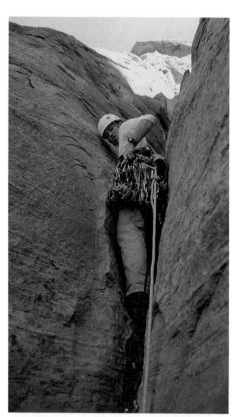

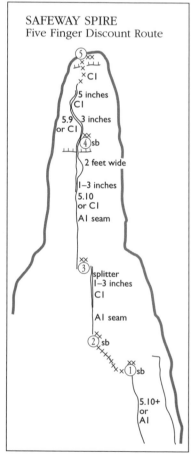

SAFEWAY SPIRE
Five Finger Discount Route

5
C1
5 inches
C1
5.9 3 inches
or C1
4 sb
2 feet wide
1–3 inches
5.10
or C1
A1 seam
3
splitter
1–3 inches
C1
A1 seam
2 sb
1 sb
5.10+
or
A1

Bryan Gall on pitch 2, the Long Dong Wall, Kissing Couple, Colorado National Monument. © Cameron M. Burns.

Climb 7, Safeway Spire, Five Finger Discount. © Cameron M. Burns.

Equipment: 2 sets of camming units with half sizes; 2 sets of small technical Friends; #5, #6, and #7 Friends; 20 small pitons of various sizes

Approach: From the Ute Canyon trailhead parking lot, follow the trail southwest toward the sandstone canyons of The Monument for about 0.5 mile or so, then turn left onto a prominent trail that leads southeast (90 degrees from the direction you were headed). Follow this trail up the back edge of a huge tilted slab, at the top of which is the entrance to Ute Canyon. Hike into Ute Canyon about 1.5 miles, and Safeway Spire becomes obvious on the right (west) side of the canyon. Start at the bottom of the east side of the tower, just left of where the tower meets the canyon wall to the north.

Route: Pitch 1: Climb up a crack/flake system (5.10+ or A1) that stops at a hanging belay. Pitch 2: Move left around the corner (C1) on a bolt ladder to a sling belay. Pitch 3: Aid the thin crack above (A1/C1), which gradually widens and ends at a sling belay. Pitch 4: Continue up the widening crack system (5.10 or C1). Pitch 5: Continue up the crack (5.9 or C1), then mantle the summit roofs on several bolts (C1).

Descent: Rappel the route.

8   OOMPAH TOWER, ETHAN PUTTERMAN AND THE CHOCOLATE FACTORY

First ascent: Cameron Burns, Jon Butler, Jesse Harvey, and Lefty Angus Burns, August 1, 1998

Difficulty: III, 5.9, C1

Time: 1 full day

Equipment: 2 sets of camming units with half sizes with #5 Camalot; 5 ⅜-inch bolt hangers

Approach: There are two ways to reach Oompah Tower; either way, one passes a prominent tower called Liberty Cap on the rim. The first way (not recommended) follows the Ute Canyon Trail southwest, toward the sandstone canyons of The Monument for about 0.5 mile or so, then turns left, onto a prominent trail that leads southeast (90 degrees from the direction you were headed). Follow this trail up the back edge of a huge tilted slab, at the top of which is the entrance to Ute Canyon. Then walk back to the west, at the same elevation, roughly 1.5 miles until a short subsidiary canyon to the south can be followed past a slender needle (Jolly Tower) to a taller, stockier tower (Oompah Tower). The second way: Once you have located Ute Canyon from the trailhead parking lot, look for the next

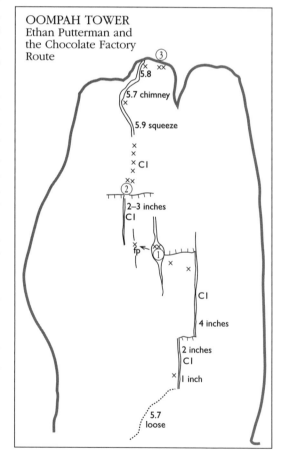

OOMPAH TOWER
Ethan Putterman and
the Chocolate Factory
Route

③
x xx
5.8
5.7 chimney
x
5.9 squeeze
x
x
x C1
x
xx
②
2–3 inches
C1
x
fp ①
x   x
C1
4 inches
2 inches
C1
x 1 inch
5.7
loose

Climb 8, Oompah Tower, Ethan Putterman and the Chocolate Factory.
© Cameron M. Burns.

canyon to the west and bushwhack up the long hill to reach it. Start at the bottom of the west side of the tower.

Route: Pitch 1: Move up and right, through loose material to the base of a splitter crack (5.7). Climb the splitter, then move left on bolts to a belay in a pod (C1). Pitch 2: Reach left, and continue up another splitter to a belay at a ledge (C1). Pitch 3: Climb the C1 bolt ladder above to an off-width crack, then follow the crack to the summit (5.9, C1).

Descent: Rappel the route.

EASTERN UTAH (MOAB AREA)

RIVER ROAD

River Road isn't really a climbing "area" as they are commonly referred to. It is simply a road—Hwy. 128—threading along the Colorado River between the ghost town of Cisco, Utah, near I-70 and Moab on US 191. Sprinkled along the road are dozens (and, likely one day, thousands) of routes. In addition to the two climbs described here, also see Castle Valley, Onion Creek Area, and Fisher Towers Area—all reached via River Road.

River Road's two finest towers—Lighthouse and Dolomite—are so stunning that they prompt reaction from any climber who has ever driven past them. Two classic routes on these spires are included here.

Area climbing regulations: The routes along River Road lie on public land, managed by the Bureau of Land Management (BLM). There are no restrictions on

Dolomite Spire and Lighthouse Tower from River Road. © Cameron M. Burns.

climbing at present, although it is up to all climbers to leave as little impact as possible so that this policy remains.

Special considerations: Watch where you park. River Road can get incredibly busy during the spring and fall seasons.

Getting there: To reach River Road from Moab, drive north on US 191 to the northern edge of town, then turn right (northeast) onto Hwy. 128, River Road. Beginning from its southwestern end (near Moab), River Road boasts mileage markers along its entirety, so it's easy to find various points along River Road. Dolomite and Lighthouse Towers, and Big Bend Butte, are 7.6 miles up River Road from US 191. They are the obvious towers and butte on the east side (right side, if you are coming from US 191) of the road.

To reach River Road from the east via I-70 from Colorado, after crossing the Utah-Colorado border, drive to exit 212, the Cisco exit, turn left under the interstate, then drive west. At about 5.7 miles, you'll pass through the old town of Cisco. Continue south and west for roughly 2.5 miles, then turn left onto Hwy. 128, River Road. Drive 37.3 miles on River Road and look for the towers and butte on the east side (left side, if you are coming from I-70) of the road.

The best place to park is in the dirt lot just off the east side of River Road, just northwest of Big Bend Butte (across the road from the BLM's Big Bend Butte camping/recreation area).

9 LIGHTHOUSE TOWER, LONELY VIGIL

First ascent: Ed Webster and Jeff Achey, September 30, 1985

Difficulty: II, 5.10-, R

Time: 1 full day

Equipment: 2 sets of Friends with 3 each of #1.5 through #3.5; 1 set of TCUs; 1 set of stoppers

Approach: From the parking lot, there are two ways to reach Lonely Vigil. The first involves hiking around Big Bend Butte to the north, then tromping up the canyon behind (east of) Big Bend Butte. There's no real trail, so staying near the creek bed is best. After passing the east side of Big Bend Butte, Lighthouse Tower (on the left) and Dolomite Spire come into view and are obvious. Or one can climb an access pitch (recommended) on the "front" side of the towers to reach them. This access pitch (5.7) climbs a

On the second pitch of Lonely Vigil, Lighthouse Tower. Photo by Rich McDonald/Widen collection.

LIGHTHOUSE TOWER
Lonely Vigil Route

DOLOMITE SPIRE
Kor Route

chimney/crack system just left on the lowest point between Lighthouse Tower and the mesa to the right (southeast). From there, hike around to the "back" of the towers. Lonely Vigil follows the most obvious, dark, top-to-bottom cleft in Lighthouse's northeast side, just right of the center of the tower.

Route: Pitch 1: Start up the obvious major cleft and climb a full rope length of hand cracks to a fixed belay (5.10-). Pitch 2: Continue straight up, over a steep corner, to a fixed belay at the notch between Lighthouse's main summit and the block to the right (northwest; 5.9). Pitch 3: Traverse left, then climb a flake to a ledge with fixed anchors just below the summit block (5.9). Pitch 4: Face-climb up the block, then mantle onto the summit (5.8 R). This last pitch requires down-climbing to the anchors atop pitch 3. It is possible to throw a rope over the summit block and rig a top rope for other climbers in your party.

Special considerations: The summit block is unprotected and, as of yet, still unbolted. Please do not add bolts to this unique summit.

Descent: Rappel the route.

10 DOLOMITE SPIRE, KOR ROUTE

First ascents: Layton Kor, Joy Kor, and Kordell Kor, April 11, 1969.
First solo ascent: Mark Whiton, May 1988.
Difficulty: III, 5.9, C2
Time: 1 full day

Northeast faces of Lighthouse Tower and Dolomite Spire, showing climb 9 (Lonely Vigil) and climb 10 (Kor Route). © Cameron M. Burns.

Rich McDonald on the second pitch of the Kor Route, Dolomite Spire. © Jeff Widen.

Equipment: 2 sets of Friends; 2 sets of TCUs; Lowe Balls; tie-offs or hangers for bolt studs

Approach: From the parking lot, there are two ways to reach the Kor Route. The first involves hiking around Big Bend Butte to the north, then tromping up the canyon behind (east of) Big Bend Butte. There's no real trail, so staying near the creek bed is best. After passing the east side of Big Bend Butte, Lighthouse Tower (on the left) and Dolomite Spire come into view and are obvious. Or one can climb an access pitch (recommended) on the "front" side of the towers to reach them. This access pitch (5.7) climbs a chimney/crack system just left on the lowest point between Lighthouse Tower and the mesa to the right (southeast). From there, hike around to the "back" of the towers. The Kor Route starts at the middle of the northeast face, then angles up and left to the notch between Lighthouse and Dolomite, then strikes out right, following cracks and bolts on the right side, as viewed from the canyon below. Start at the bottom of the northeast side of the tower.

Route: Pitch 1: Climb up easy Class 5 rock through a chimney to the ridgeline between Dolomite Spire and Lighthouse Tower. Pitch 2: Climb C2+ cracks leading up and right (northeast) to a belay. Pitch 3: Climb bolts and cracks to an overhanging bolt ladder, then a belay on a decent ledge (C2). Pitch 4: Traverse right, to the ridge between Dolomite and Big Bend Butte, then ascend the ridge via face-climbing (5.9). Belay from fixed anchors at the base of a blank face (to prevent rope drag). Pitch 5: Continue up using bolts (C1) and free-climbing (5.8) to the top.

Special considerations: Bolts and their "hangers" on this route have historically been pretty sketchy. A bolt kit (for replacing them) and hanger replacements can be helpful. Besides those considerations, the route goes clean.

Descent: Rappel from the summit to a stance with anchors on Big Bend Butte, the mesa next to the tower, then from the stance to the ground.

CASTLE VALLEY

Castle Valley is a large, wide, sprawling desert valley located roughly 20 road miles northeast of Moab, Utah. Pushed hard up against the northeastern side of the La Sal Mountains, and sitting at 5,000 feet elevation, the spires and buttes of Castle Valley are, in many ways, where desert climbing begins for many young climbers.

Every spring and fall, hundreds of neophyte desert climbers from across the country and around the world make the pilgrimage to Castleton Tower to try what has become the standard beginner's desert route, the Kor-Ingalls.

In recent years, the total ascent tally has been estimated at more than 4,000 on the conservative side and 7,000 on the liberal side. Yet, while the Kor-Ingalls route is often crowded, it can also be completely vacant during a weekday in midsummer or midwinter.

Certainly, the Kor-Ingalls is a good route, but it receives far more attention than it should, considering that there are excellent routes just around the corner from the Kor-Ingalls, as well as on the neighboring buttes and spires in Castle Valley. The Wingate sandstone found here is extremely solid, and the popularity of climbing in the area means that fixed anchors are regularly replaced.

Area climbing regulations: The routes in Castle Valley lie on public land, managed by the Bureau of Land Management (BLM). There are no restrictions on climbing at present, although it is up to all climbers to leave as little impact as possible so that this policy remains.

Special considerations: The unique deposits of calcite that occur in the cracks and chimneys of Castle Valley can make for extremely painful climbing, especially anyplace where there are squeeze chimneys and off-widths. Clothing that can save your tender skin from these hazards is recommended. Likewise, the calcite can be just as hard on ropes and fabric, something to be aware of when you are leading a pitch where the rope runs against edges and in cracks.

Also, Castle Valley's high winds are notorious, and can easily wrap the free ends of ropes around flakes and edges that are impossible to reach. Descents in windy conditions, therefore, can be the cruxes of routes in Castle Valley, and caution is advised not to let your rope get hung up.

Getting there: Castle Valley is best reached via Hwy. 128, more commonly known as River Road. This road runs northeast-southwest along the southern side of the Colorado River between Moab and the settlement of Cisco, which sits along the south side of I-70, near the Colorado border.

From Moab, drive north until River Road becomes obvious on the right. It is well marked and especially easy to follow because the road boasts mileage markers. Most climbers use these mileage markers to locate and describe climbs. Follow River Road for about 15.5 miles and turn right, onto the Castle Valley Road. In recent years, Castle Valley has become an expensive suburban development, partly because of the stunning views of the towers in Castle Valley. Follow Castle Valley Road for 4.7 miles to a dirt road leading left. Drive just a short distance up this road to a designated BLM parking area.

From the east (Colorado) via I-70 and Cisco, take I-70 exit 212. Turn left under the interstate and immediately turn right, onto a frontage road. This is a good place to zero out your odometer. Follow the bouncy frontage road southwest through the ghost town of Cisco (at about 5.7 miles from exit 212), then continue to the intersection with River Road (Hwy. 128) at 8.3 miles. Turn left onto River Road and follow it to the Castle Valley Road at 28 miles from exit 212. Follow Castle Valley Road for 4.7 miles, to a dirt road leading left. Drive just a short distance up this road to the designated BLM parking area.

All the Castle Valley routes in this guidebook are best approached via the Castleton Tower Trail, with the exception of Jah Man on Sister Superior (climb 19) and the Longbow Chimney on Crooked Arrow Spire (climb 20). Access to those routes is described below. The Castleton Tower Trail leaves the parking lot and heads roughly north, into a shallow slot canyon, then winds around a bit and finally comes out on the mesa below Castleton's notorious talus cone. Follow the trail up the talus cone to reach Castleton Tower, The Rectory, The Nuns, and The Priest.

The best way to reach Sister Superior and Crooked Arrow Spire from Moab is to drive 1.3 miles northeast on Hwy. 128 (River Road) past the Castle Valley Road (the turnoff to Castleton and The Priest), and pull off and park on the south side of the road. From the east, drive on Hwy. 128 (River Road) 26.7 miles from exit 212 on I-70, and pull off and park on the south side of the road. There is an old dirt road (currently closed) that leads from Hwy. 128 south into Ida Gulch, the valley between Parriott Mesa and the Convent, two huge mesas on either side of Ida Gulch. Sister Superior, a slender needle of sandstone, is visible to the southeast on the same ridge as Castleton Tower, The Rectory, The Priest, and The Nuns. A well-used trail leads south into the valley, then switchbacks up the hill to Sister Superior. Crooked Arrow Spire lies across Ida Gulch from Sister Superior and is the obvious slender needle sprouting from Parriott Mesa.

11 CASTLETON TOWER, KOR-INGALLS

First ascents: Layton Kor and Huntley Ingalls, September 15, 1961.
First solo ascent: Mark Hesse, 1977.
Difficulty: III, 5.9
Time: 1 full day
Equipment: 2 sets of Camalots; medium stoppers
Approach: From the parking lot, the Castleton Tower Trail heads roughly north into a shallow slot canyon, winds around a bit, and comes out on the mesa below Castleton Tower's notorious talus cone. Castleton Tower is the slender, red tower standing by itself; hike to its base. The Kor-Ingalls route follows the huge dihedral system on the southeast side of the tower, the easiest-looking line of ascent.
Route: Pitch 1: Climb up a short corner (5.6) to a huge ledge and belay on the ledge at a fixed anchor. There are several variations, all about the same grade. Pitch 2: Start up a pair of parallel cracks and move right, into the right-hand crack (5.8). Continue up to a small ledge with fixed anchors. Pitch 3: Shimmy up the scary-looking off-width (5.9-) past a bolt to a good ledge and fixed anchors. Pitch 4: Climb up toward the notch between the main tower and a detached flake, then move up and left (5.7) on fun edges to the summit.

Climb 11, Castleton Tower, Kor-Ingalls. © Cameron M. Burns.

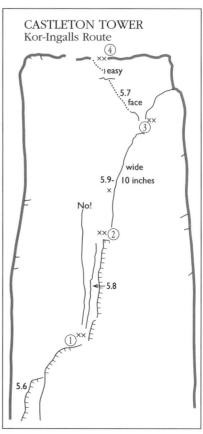

CASTLETON TOWER
Kor-Ingalls Route

④

easy

5.7
face

③ ××

wide
5.9- / 10 inches
×

No!

×× ②

← 5.8

① ××

5.6

Leading the last pitch of the Kor-Ingalls Route, Castleton Tower, Castle Valley. © Cameron M. Burns.

Special considerations: This route can be very crowded. A helmet is a must. Also, wide gear (#4 Big Bros or the equivalent) can be helpful, but most parties do the route without it.

Descent: Rappel the route using fixed anchors, or rappel the North Face Standard Route (climb 13) if the Kor-Ingalls route is clogged with traffic.

12   CASTLETON TOWER, NORTH CHIMNEY

First ascent: Dan Burgette and Allen Erickson, April 1, 1970
Difficulty: III, 5.9-
Time: 1 full day
Equipment: 2 sets of Camalots; medium stoppers; something large to
  protect the 9-inch off-width on the second pitch
Approach: From the parking lot, take the Castleton Tower Trail to the mesa
below Castleton Tower's talus cone. Castleton Tower is the slender, red tower stand-

ing by itself. From the southeast side of the tower (the Kor-Ingalls route, climb 11), walk counterclockwise around the tower (to the right, from the Kor-Ingalls route) to the obvious cleft that splits the tower top to bottom and faces toward The Rectory. This is the North Chimney.

Route: Pitch 1: Climb up a huge, slightly overhanging corner with perfect 5.8+ hand jams for 160 feet and belay in a small alcove. Pitch 2: Continue straight up the off-width above (5.9) past a bolt to easier ground, and belay in the back of the chimney. Pitch 3: Continue up the chimney (5.8) to the notch between a large detached flake and the main tower, and belay in the notch. Pitch 4: Same as pitch 4 of the Kor-Ingalls route: Climb up toward the notch between the main tower and a detached flake, them move up and left (5.7) on fun edges to the summit.

Special considerations: This route can be very windy and cold in winter.

Descent: Rappel the Kor-Ingalls route (climb 11) or the North Face Standard Route (climb 13) using fixed anchors.

13 CASTLETON TOWER, NORTH FACE STANDARD ROUTE

First ascents: Jim Dunn and Doug Snively, March 20, 1974 (with some aid). *First free ascent:* Ed Webster and Buck Norden, April 16, 1979 (they added the first-pitch corner, to the point where the route underclings to the right). *Second free ascent:* Bruce Lella and Bob Rotert, 1980 (they added the "undercling right" variation, creating the modern classic).

Difficulty: III, 5.11-

Time: 1 full day

Equipment: 3 sets of Friends in the #1.5 to #3.5 range; #4 Camalot; 1 set of TCUs; medium stoppers

Approach: From the parking lot, take the Castleton Tower Trail to the mesa below Castleton Tower's talus cone. Castleton Tower is the slender, red tower standing by itself; hike to its base. From the southeast side of the tower (the Kor-Ingalls route, climb 11), walk counterclockwise around the tower (to the right, from the Kor-Ingalls route) to the obvious cleft that splits the tower top to bottom and faces toward The Rectory. This is the

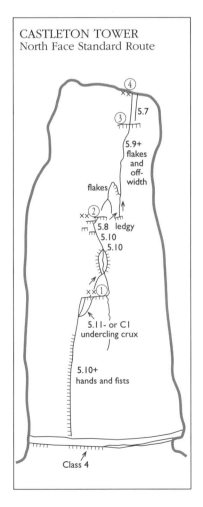

CASTLETON TOWER
North Face Standard Route

④
5.7
③
5.9+
flakes
and
off-
width
flakes
②
5.8 ledgy
5.10
5.10
①
5.11- or C1
undercling crux
5.10+
hands and fists
Class 4

North Chimney. From the North Chimney, continue counterclockwise around the tower for about 100 feet to the base of the north face. There are several obvious crack systems here. The North Face Standard Route begins in the obvious, deep, right-facing corner with a hand crack in the back of it, farthest left on the face. Scramble up to the base of the corner to start the route.

Route: Pitch 1: Climb a hand and fist crack in a right-facing corner (5.10+) past a small roof, then undercling right (5.11- or C1) to a belay stance with chain anchors. Pitch 2: Climb a 5.9 finger crack into an alcove (the "Pod," a weird hole in the crack), then over a small roof (5.10) and up flakes and edges to a fixed anchor. Pitch 3: Traverse to the right from the belay up flakes and edges to an off-width/chimney system (5.9+), then continue up the off-width above to a fixed belay. Pitch 4: Climb an easy chimney (5.7) to the summit.

Special considerations: This route can be very windy and cold in winter.

Descent: Rappel the route or the Kor-Ingalls route (climb 11) using fixed anchors. Many climbers use this route as a descent when the Kor-Ingalls is clogged with traffic.

14 THE RECTORY, FINE JADE

> **First ascent:** Chip Chace and Pat Ellinwood, 1984
> **Difficulty:** III, 5.11
> **Time:** 1 full day
> **Equipment:** 3 sets of Friends from #1 to #2.5; #4 Camalot; 1 set of TCUs or the equivalent; medium stoppers
> **Approach:** From the parking lot, take the Castleton Tower Trail to Castleton Tower, the slender, red tower standing by itself. North of Castleton is a long, flat-topped mesa, The Rectory. After reaching Castleton's base, hike north to the southern end of The Rectory, where Fine Jade lies. It follows the obvious crack system splitting the southern end of The Rectory. Scramble up to the base of the crack system.
> **Route:** Pitch 1: Climb an off-width and fist crack (5.10+) up over a bulge, then a small roof, and continue to a stance with fixed anchors. Pitch 2: Climb the thin crack above the belay past a horizontal crack to a decent ledge (5.11-). Pitch 3: Climb up and right, on edges and flakes to a short, left-facing corner (5.9), then continue over a bulge to a ledge with fixed anchors. Pitch 4: Climb a short, left-facing corner, then move up and right and face-climb (5.11-) past several bolts to the summit.
> **Special considerations:** There is some loose rock on this route.
> **Descent:** Rappel the route.

15 THE RECTORY, CRACK WARS

> **First ascent:** Glen Randall and Charlie Fowler, October 1982
> **Difficulty:** III, 5.11
> **Time:** 1 full day
> **Equipment:** 2 sets of camming units to #5 Camalot, with extra #4; 1 set of TCUs
> **Approach:** From the parking lot, take the Castleton Tower Trail to Castleton Tower, the slender, red tower standing by itself. North of Castleton is a long, flat-

Climb 14, The Rectory, Fine Jade. © Cameron M. Burns.

topped mesa, The Rectory. After reaching Castleton's base, hike north to the southern end of The Rectory. Crack Wars follows the most obvious splitter on the northwestern end of The Rectory, just 150 feet right of the right Nun.

Route: Pitch 1: Move around the right side of a block at the base of the crack, then climb the crack (5.10+ hands/fists) to a sling belay. Pitch 2: Continue up the widening crack (5.10 off-width) to a sling belay. Pitch 3: Climb 5.9 hand cracks to a left-angling slot (5.11), then a belay. Pitch 4: A 5.9 finger crack in a right-facing corner leads to the summit.

Special considerations: There is much painful calcite. Check out the descent before you climb.

Climb 15, The Rectory, Crack Wars. © Cameron M. Burns.

Descent: Walk to the northern end of The Rectory, then rappel the Empirical Route, which lies 100 feet left of Crack Wars, in the corner between The Nuns and The Rectory.

16 THE PRIEST, HONEYMOON CHIMNEY

First ascents: Layton Kor, Fred Beckey, Harvey Carter, and Annie Carter, September 16–17, 1961. *First free ascent:* Robert Warren and John Catto, 1980. *First solo ascent:* Jeff Widen, November 15, 1986.
Difficulty: III, 5.11- or 5.9, C1
Time: 1 full day
Equipment: 1 set of Friends with half sizes; 2 #4 Big Bros

Approach: From the parking lot, take the Castleton Tower Trail to Castleton Tower, the slender, red tower standing by itself. North of Castleton is a long, flat-topped mesa, The Rectory. The Priest is the freestanding tower at the far northern end of The Rectory. After reaching Castleton's base, head north along the western side of The Rectory. The Priest, a large tower separated from the northern end of The Rectory, is obvious. Honeymoon Chimney is the large crack system splitting the entire Priest from bottom to top on the west side of the tower.

Route: Pitch 1: Climb the left side of a 15-foot block sitting at the base of the tower, then squeeze and arm-bar up the off-width/squeeze chimney above (5.9) until it's possible to worm your way into the chimney splitting the tower. Belay at a fixed anchor. Pitch 2: Facing south, chimney and stem straight up for 40 feet (5.7) past an old bolt, and gradually move up and right (west), to the edge of the chimney.

Southwest faces of The Priest (climb 16, Honeymoon Chimney) and The Rectory (climb 15, Crack Wars, and climb 14, Fine Jade). © Cameron M. Burns.

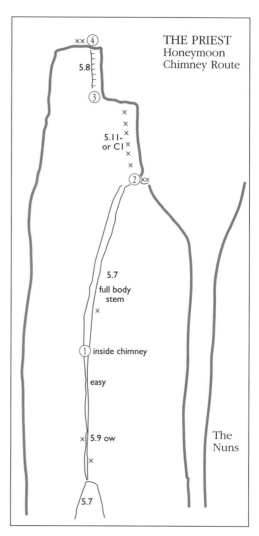

THE PRIEST
Honeymoon
Chimney Route

5.8

5.11-
or C1

5.7
full body
stem

① inside chimney

easy

5.9 ow

5.7

The
Nuns

Ed Webster on the crux bolt ladder of The Priest's Honeymoon Chimney. Photo by Patrick Griffin/ Ed Webster collection.

(There is reportedly another bolt out near the west, right, edge of the chimney, but it's hard to find.) Belay on the subsidiary summit on the south, at a stance with fixed anchors. Pitch 3: Climb the widening chimney above, then step across to the main tower and face-climb (5.11- or C1) past the bolt ladder on a sharp arête. At the top of the bolt ladder, move up and left to a ledge with fixed anchors. Pitch 4: Climb up and left to a shallow left-facing corner (5.8) and the summit.

Special considerations: As with many other desert routes, on the first and second pitches over the years, various bolts have appeared and been removed. A friend recently reported that there are now three bolts protecting the first lead, and two protecting the second pitch (although the second bolt on the second pitch is far to the west and hard to find.) Expect all these bolts to be removed or more added at any time.

Descent: Rappel the route using fixed anchors.

17 THE NUNS, HOLIER THAN THOU

First ascent: Jay Smith and Mark Hesse, 1995 (pitch 3 was first climbed by John Catto, Jay Smith, and Mark Hesse as part of Bad Habit, climb 18, a few days prior to the first ascent of Holier Than Thou)
Difficulty: II, 5.11c
Time: 1 full day
Equipment: 14 quickdraws

Approach: From the parking lot, take the Castleton Tower Trail to Castleton Tower, the slender, red tower standing by itself. North of Castleton is a long, flat-topped mesa, The Rectory. The Priest is the free-standing tower at the far northern end of The Rectory, and huddled between The Rectory and The Priest is the twin-summitted Nuns. After reaching Castleton's base, head north along the western side of The Rectory to The Priest, a large tower separated from the northern end of The Rectory. Once below the west face of The Priest, walk around the corner to the cold northeast faces of the rock formations, then scramble up to The Priest's east face. Directly south, on the white-pocketed calcite wall of the

North face of The Nuns: climb 18, Bad Habit, and climb 17, Holier Than Thou. © Cameron M. Burns.

northern Nun (which faces The Priest) is the Holier Than Thou route. Bolts are hard to see until you are quite close.

Route: Pitch 1: Climb a bolt-protected 5.11c pitch to a fixed belay. Pitch 2: Climb a runout 5.9+ face to a fixed belay. Pitch 3: Scramble to the top.

Descent: Down-climb to top of pitch 2; rappel the route.

18　THE NUNS, BAD HABIT

First ascent: John Catto, Jay Smith, and Mark Hesse, 1995

Difficulty: II, 5.11c

Time: 1 full day

Equipment: 2 sets of Friends; 2 sets of small stoppers

Approach: From the parking lot, take the Castleton Tower Trail to Castleton Tower, the slender, red tower standing by itself. North of Castleton is a long, flat-topped mesa, The Rectory. The Priest is the freestanding tower at the far northern end of The Rectory, and huddled between The Rectory and The Priest is the twin-summitted Nuns. After reaching Castleton's base, head north along the western side of The Rectory to The Priest, a large tower separated from the northern end of The Rectory. Once below the west face of The Priest, walk around the corner to the cold northeast faces of the rock formations, then scramble up to The Priest's east face. Directly south, on the white-pocketed calcite wall of the northern Nun (which faces The Priest) is Holier Than Thou (climb 17). Bad Habit climbs a left-facing corner just left of Holier Than Thou.

Route: Pitch 1: Climb thin hands/fingers up the back of the flaring corner to a fixed belay (5.11c). Pitch 2: Continue straight up to another fixed belay (5.10-). Pitch 3: Scramble to the top.

Special considerations: This route is better than it looks.

Descent: Down-climb to top of pitch 2; rappel the route.

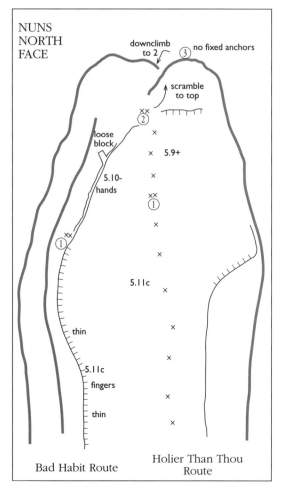

NUNS NORTH FACE

downclimb to 2 — ③ no fixed anchors

scramble to top

XX ② ⊤⊤⊤⊤⊤

loose block

5.10- hands

x

x 5.9+

x

XX ①

x

XX ①

x

x

5.11c x

x

thin

x

5.11c fingers

x

thin

x

Bad Habit Route

Holier Than Thou Route

19 SISTER SUPERIOR, JAH MAN

First ascent: Ken Trout and Kirk Miller, 1984
Difficulty: III, 5.10+
Time: 1 full day
Equipment: 3 sets of Camalots to #3; 2 0.75 Camalots; 2 0.5 Camalots

Approach: From the old dirt road into Ida Gulch, take the well-used trail that leads south into the valley, switchbacking up the hill on the west side of Sister Superior. Jah Man starts at the far left (northwest) side at the base of the southwest face, which is a flat, ironlike face coated with much white calcite.

Route: Pitch 1: Climb up broken ledges 20 feet (5.9) and move to the right on the loose ledge for 40 feet to the base of the obvious chimney. Climb the chimney

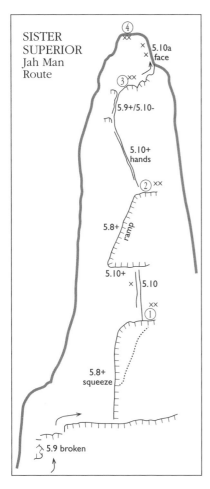

Climb 19, Sister Superior, Jah Man.
© Cameron M. Burns.

Jordan Campbell following pitch 2, Jah Man, Sister Superior, Castle Valley. © Cameron M. Burns.

(5.8+) to a good ledge at the top of a large flake and a fixed anchor. Pitch 2: Continue straight up from the belay on thin hand cracks, pass an old bolt, then move left (5.10+) under a small roof. Mantle the roof and scramble up the easy ramp above (5.8+) for 50 feet. Pitch 3: Climb thin but solid hand cracks up and left (5.10+), turn the corner, and continue up a thin hand crack (5.9+–5.10-) to a spacious ledge with a fixed belay. Pitch 4: Step right, clamber up the boulder, then face-climb (5.10a) past several bolts to the flat, spacious summit and a large rappel anchor.

Special considerations: The first pitch is often done as two separate pitches, with the 5.8+ chimney being the second pitch. Many parties do both pitches as one. Also, the 5.8+ chimney features a healthy coating of calcite and is extraordinarily painful to climb because of its narrowness. Climbers with large body appendages should tape up!

Descent: Rappel the route from fixed anchors. The descent has been described in some guidebooks as possible with one 165-foot rope. It is, with the exception of the last rappel, from the top of the 5.8+ chimney to the ground. That rappel requires two ropes, or else down-climbing the very short first pitch.

20 CROOKED ARROW SPIRE, LONGBOW CHIMNEY

First ascents: Harvey Carter and Ken Wyrick, September 1974. *First solo ascent:* Peter Gallagher, 1985.

Difficulty: III, 5.8, C1

Time: 1 full day

Equipment: 2 sets of Friends; 2 sets of stoppers; tie-offs for the old bolt ladder

Approach: From the old dirt road into Ida Gulch, take the well-used trail that leads south into the valley, switchbacking up the hill on the west side of Sister Superior and the other pinnacles surrounding it. As you begin hiking into Ida Gulch, Crooked Arrow Spire is the obvious thin tower (sprouting from Parriott Mesa behind it) on your right. Leave the Sister Superior trail as you near Parriott Mesa's talus cone on the mesa's northeast side (about 5 minutes from the car). Hike up cliff bands to the base of the tower. The Longbow Chimney starts on the left (south) side of the tower when viewed from below.

Route: Pitch 1: Climb the obvious chimney left of the base of the spire toward the notch between the spire and the mesa behind (5.8). Pitch 2: Climb the spire via a thin crack and long bolt ladder. (C1).

Descent: Rappel the route.

ONION CREEK AREA

Onion Creek is a beautiful little stream that drains into the general Fisher Towers area from high up in the La Sal Mountains. The road winding along the creek's edge is a fantastic drive through the geologic strata of the Cutler sandstone of the area, cresting in a high valley on the north side of the La Sals. There are many towers in this area but, to date, only two have reached that immortal status of "classic": The Hindu and The Doric Column.

Although they are similar in nature to the Fisher Towers, the towers along Onion Creek are perhaps more beautiful because, unlike the fin-shaped Fisher Towers, The Hindu and The Doric Column are real towers: thin cylinders of red rock stretching up into the sky like buildings in a bizarre city. The best thing about them for climbers is that these formations see probably a tenth the traffic that the routes in the Fisher Towers do, so if your climb in the Fishers has a waiting line, go check out Onion Creek.

Area climbing regulations: The routes in the Onion Creek area lie on public land, managed by the Bureau of Land Management (BLM). There are no restrictions on climbing at present, although it is up to all climbers to leave as little impact as possible so that this policy remains.

Special considerations: As with climbs in the Fisher Towers, the routes in Onion Creek are as serious as anything in the desert. Extreme caution, solid knowledge of tricky aid- and free-climbing techniques, and a healthy respect for loose rock are prerequisites for climbing here.

Getting there: The simplest way to get to Onion Creek is via River Road toward the Fisher Towers. From Moab, drive north on US 191, then turn right (northeast) onto Hwy. 128, also known as River Road. Follow River Road for 21.7 miles, past Castle Valley and Castleton Tower, and 0.9 mile before the turnoff for the Fisher Towers. From the east, via I-70 from Colorado, after crossing the Utah-Colorado border, drive to exit 212, the Cisco exit, turn left under the interstate, then drive west. At about 5.7 miles, pass through the old town of Cisco. Continue south and west for roughly 2.5 miles, then turn left onto Hwy. 128 (River Road). Follow this for 23.5 miles, exactly 0.9 mile past the turnoff for the Fisher Towers. The Onion Creek road leads off to the southeast, and there is a sign at this intersection stating "Taylor Fisher Valley Ranch." (Do not confuse this road with another dirt road lying to the southeast with a similar sign, which states "Taylor Creek Ranch." That road will not get you to Onion Creek.)

Take the Onion Creek road and follow it for 3.3 miles (four-wheel drive recommended but not necessary); to reach The Hindu, park on the left side of the road. The slender spire is obvious to the south across the creek. To reach The Doric Column, drive past this parking spot for The Hindu for another 1.2 miles and park. The Doric Column lies up the hillside left (east) of the road, and can be accessed by any number of routes.

21 THE HINDU, MAVERICK

First ascents: Harvey Carter and Steve Merrill, April 16, 1964. *First solo ascent:* Jon Butler, Fall 1994. *First free and clean ascent:* Stevie Haston and Laurence Gouault, April 1996.

Difficulty: II–III, 5.13a or III, 5.8, A2

Time: ½ day

Equipment: 2 sets of wired stoppers with extra medium stoppers; 2 sets of Camalots; 3 knifeblades; 3 Lost Arrows; 2 ⅝-inch angles

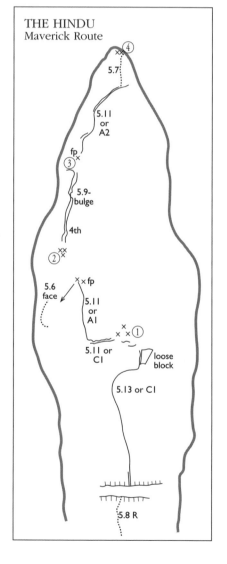

THE HINDU
Maverick Route

Approach: From where you parked, hike north up low-angled slabs and benches to the base of the tower, then out along a "land bridge" leading to the southwest face of The Hindu. The Maverick route follows the thin crack system that faces the land bridge.

Route: Pitch 1: Climb rotten 5.8 R rock for 30 feet to a large ledge with an obvious clean crack above it. Continue up the crack for 60 feet (5.13 or C1) to a hanging belay. Pitch 2: Move left along a horizontal crack 15 feet, then climb a thin crack to a fixed pendulum point (5.11 or A1). Pendulum left to easier ground, then scramble up to a three-bolt belay. Pitch 3: Climb easy ground up to a bulging roof (5.9-), continue over another bulge (5.7), then move up and left to a flat ledge and a fixed belay. Pitch 4: Climb up into the small curving roof above the belay and either free-climb or aid (5.11 or A2) over it to easier ground above. Continue up and to the right to a ledge, then mantle onto the summit.

Special considerations: The route has been free-climbed, but most parties still aid their way up it. Pitches 1 and 2 can be joined together to eliminate an uncomfortable hanging belay. Likewise, pitches 3 and 4 can be linked together. However, joining any of the pitches together can result in massive rope drag. Also, be careful going around the loose flake near the top of the first pitch. It's ready to drop off. If it hasn't already, the route will likely go clean in the near future. It's 98 percent clean now.

Descent: Make one double-rope rappel down the southwest face from fixed anchors at the summit.

22 THE DORIC COLUMN, SOUTHEAST CHIMNEY

First ascents: Bill Forrest, George Hurley, and Rod Chuck, April 1969. *First free ascent:* Mike Pennings, February 1999.
Difficulty: IV, 5.8, A2+ or IV, 5.11-
Time: 1 full day
Equipment: 2 sets of camming units; 2 sets of TCUs; a selection of small pitons; many carabiners and slings. Also, much of the route is a bolt ladder, so bring tie-offs/ extra stoppers/hangers for hangerless bolts.

Approach: From where you parked, The Doric Column, which is up the hillside left (east) of the road, can be accessed by a number of routes. The simplest way to reach it is to examine the surrounding landscape. To the south (right, when viewed from the road), the terrain is a series of broken hills and sandy mesas. To the north (left, when viewed from the road) is the start of the rugged Cutler sandstone canyons that dominate the area. Hike up the slot canyon (Class 3–4) that divides the two types of landscapes. After an hour's hiking uphill, the Mystery Towers come into view. The Doric

Climb 21, The Hindu, Maverick.
© Cameron M. Burns.

On pitch 3, Southeast Chimney, Doric Column, Onion Creek. Photo: Butler collection.

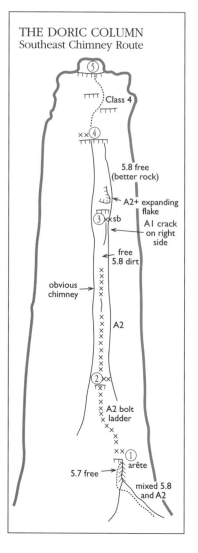

THE DORIC COLUMN
Southeast Chimney Route

Class 4

5.8 free
(better rock)

A2+ expanding
flake
sb
A1 crack
on right
side

free
5.8 dirt

obvious
chimney

A2

A2 bolt
ladder

arête
5.7 free

mixed 5.8
and A2

Column is the slender cylinder behind the other towers, closest to the mesa wall behind. The southeast chimney lies on the uphill side of the tower.

Route: Pitch 1: Starting at the shoulder on the southeast side of the tower, climb mixed 5.8 and A2 rock up to an arête that ends at a small belay ledge. Pitch 2: Climb a bolt ladder in the chimney above the first belay to a cramped belay inside the chimney (A2). Pitch 3: Continue up the bolt ladder to the end of the bolts, then free-climb (5.8) the muddy chimney above. Above the chimney, aid up a good crack (A1) to a hanging belay. Pitch 4: Make several free moves off the belay to gain a flake system. Aid up the flake system to good rock and easier climbing, then a good belay ledge (5.8, A2+). Pitch 5: Continue Class 4 climbing to the summit.

Special considerations: As with other Fisher Towers/Mystery Towers routes, all bolts should be treated as suspect. On the free ascent, the route was climbed in two pitches up to the base of pitch 5. Both pitches are rated 5.11-.

Descent: Down-climb pitch 5 to the top of pitch 4. Make two rappels down the route from the tops of pitches 4 and 2.

FISHER TOWERS AREA

Wild mud curtains. Gnarled and twisted rock knobs. Frighteningly loose grit. Sketchy gear. Air clogged with dust.

Welcome to the Fisher Towers, possibly the most challenging area for rock climbing in the desert Southwest. If you get good here, you can go climbing almost anywhere in the world and feel pretty comfortable on any kind of ground, including desperate alpine terrain.

The Fisher Towers from the parking lot. The large tower on the left is the Kingfisher. The summit furthest right is the Titan. Just left of the Titan, with the rounded knob on its top, is Cottontail Tower. The big tower left of Cottontail is Echo Tower. Directly below Cottontail's summit is the "Corkscrew Summit" of Ancient Art (in shadow).
© Cameron M. Burns.

While the Fisher Towers do carry a heavy reputation for being every climber's worst nightmare, there are many routes that—if you don't mind at least a little dust in your eyes—would qualify as classics anywhere in the world. Indeed, the Stolen Chimney route on Ancient Art has become one of the best-loved classic routes in the Southwest, because of its easy climbing, big exposure, and wild summit. This isn't the only classic route; there are many. Check them out, but don't hurry: You'll want to build up years of experience before you tackle some of the longer routes.

Although technically River Tower is not a part of the Fisher Towers and lies

along River Road just to the north of the Fisher Towers, it has more in common with the Fisher Towers than most other routes along River Road, and it is so close to the Fisher Towers that it is included in this chapter.

Area climbing regulations: The routes in the Fisher Towers lie on public land, managed by the Bureau of Land Management (BLM). There are no restrictions on climbing at present, although it is up to all climbers to leave as little impact as possible so that this policy remains.

Special considerations: The routes in the Fisher Towers are as serious as anything in the desert. Extreme caution, solid knowledge of tricky aid- and free-climbing techniques, and a healthy respect for loose rock are prerequisites for climbing in the Fishers. Also, a big thick helmet should be considered part of any rack for routes in the Fishers.

Getting there: The Fisher Towers are located near the eastern end of Castle Valley, about 20 miles northeast of Moab, Utah.

To reach the Fisher Towers from Moab, drive north on US 191, then turn right (northeast)

Lizard Rock, Fisher Towers. Photo: Webster collection.

onto Hwy. 128, known locally as River Road because it follows the Colorado River. Beginning from its southwestern end (near Moab), River Road boasts mileage markers along its entirety, so it's easy to find various points along River Road. Follow River Road for 22.6 miles, past Castle Valley and Castleton Tower. The Fisher Towers come into sight to the southeast. At 22.6 miles, at a dirt road leading to the Fisher Towers, there is a sign stating "Fisher Tower." Turn right and follow this dirt road for 1.4 miles to the Fisher Towers parking lot.

To reach the Fisher Towers from the east, via I-70 from Colorado, after crossing the Utah-Colorado border, drive to exit 212, the Cisco exit, turn left under the interstate, then drive west. At about 5.7 miles, you'll pass through the old town of Cisco. Continue south and west for roughly 2.5 miles, then turn left onto Hwy. 128 (River Road). Follow this for 22.2 miles, turn left, and drive 1.4 miles to the Fisher Towers parking lot.

Routes 23–30 are accessed via the Titan Trail, a dirt track that wanders south from the parking lot and skirts around the western edges of some of the major towers. After about a 0.5-mile hike, the first towers one comes to are the Ancient Art complex and, behind it up the hill a few hundred yards, the Kingfisher. There is a well-worn climbers track leading up to the base of Ancient Art and the Kingfisher, along their southern sides (the right side when viewed from the trail). This trail is getting so much use from climbers that today many tourists follow it, thinking it's the main trail.

To reach River Tower from Moab, simply drive northeast along River Road for exactly 2.1 miles past the Fisher Towers turnoff and turn right, onto a small, unmarked dirt road that heads vaguely toward River Tower. Follow this road for about 0.5 mile, and park near a large tree. River Tower is obvious off to the right (southeast).

To reach River Tower from the northeast (Colorado), follow directions to the Fisher Towers turnoff. Then turn around and head back up River Road for 2.1 miles, until you reach the small dirt road on the right (this road is very easy to miss when coming from the northeast). Follow the dirt road for 0.5 mile or so, and park. River Tower is obvious off to the southeast and is a 45-minute hike.

23 LIZARD ROCK, ENTRY FEE

First ascent: Harvey and Annie Carter, June 1, 1962
Difficulty: I, 5.8
Time: 10 minutes
Equipment: 1 #4 Camalot

Approach: From the Fisher Towers parking lot, walk east over a small rise, and Lizard Rock should be obvious. It is the 50-foot, thin tower closest to the parking lot.

Route: Start at the base of the west side of the tower and climb up and right where the west and south faces meet (5.7) to a ledge below the capstone. Mantle the capstone (5.8).

Special considerations: Several super-contrived variations are possible. Protection is poor.

Descent: Make one rappel down the west face from fixed anchors on the summit.

24 ANCIENT ART, STOLEN CHIMNEY (A.K.A. CORKSCREW SUMMIT)

First ascents: Paul Sibley and Bill Roos, April 29, 1969. *First free ascent:* Keith Reynolds and Burton Moomaw, May 1991.

Difficulty: II, 5.11a or II, 5.9, C1

Time: 3–4 hours

Equipment: 1 set of wired stoppers; 1 set of Camalots (mostly this route is protected by clipping fixed gear)

Approach: From the Fisher Towers parking lot, follow the Titan Trail for about 0.5 mile, until the four-summitted Ancient Art complex comes into view above the trail. From the Titan Trail, hike up a trail leading east, then north. Stolen Chimney is obvious as the last crack system to the left, on the southwest face of the Ancient Art complex.

Route: Pitch 1: From below the southwest side of the tower, scramble up crumbling ledges (5.5) to the base of a washed-out gully with four bolts leading up it. Climb the bolt ladder (most parties yard on slings) to a sloping stance with a several-bolt anchor (5.11a or 5.8, C1). Pitch 2: Climb the fun 5.7 chimney above to its top and step right, onto a large ledge with a three-bolt anchor. Pitch 3: Climb over the block at the top of the chimney, then scramble up over several smaller blocks and past three bolts (5.9) that lead to a belay anchor that is just out of sight from the ledge at the top of pitch 2. Pitch 4: Walk out the bridge to the "Diving Board" (the huge point of rock jutting south, back toward the belay), clip a bolt on its end, then work left past the Diving Board to several delicate 5.9 face moves that lead up and right to a ledge with a fixed bolt. Stand on the ledge, clip the bolt above, and mantle onto the sloping summit block. (To reach the summit of Ancient Art from the top of pitch 3, most climbers go

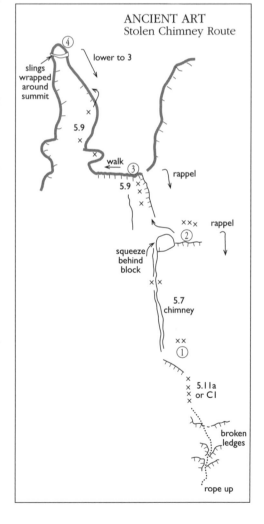

ANCIENT ART
Stolen Chimney Route

South face of Ancient Art: climb 24, Stolen Chimney, and climb 25, Hippie Route.
© Cameron M. Burns.

one at a time from the belay, climb to the top, then lower off and walk back along the bridge, and back to the belay at the top of pitch 3. From here, the descent proper begins.

Special considerations: The route gets horrendous amounts of traffic, so extreme caution (and a helmet) are required.

Descent: From the top of pitch 3, one short rappel down the ridge gets you to the large ledge at the top of the chimney. Then make one single-rope rappel followed by a double-rope rappel down the route.

25 ANCIENT ART, HIPPIE ROUTE

> **First ascents:** Herbie Hendricks and Dennis Willis, June 6–11, 1967.
> *First free ascent:* Harvey Carter and Tim Jennings, November 1967.
> **Difficulty:** II–III, 5.10+
> **Time:** 4 hours
> **Equipment:** 2 sets of Camalots with 2 #5s; a few thin pitons can help to protect pitch 4

Approach: See the approach and pitch 1 for climb 24, Stolen Chimney. From the bench below the first four bolts on Stolen Chimney, walk right 200 feet, onto a sandy slope. Belay here; there are no fixed anchors.

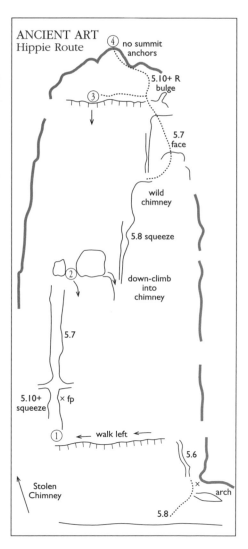

Pitch 2, Hippie Route, Ancient Art, Fisher Towers. © Cameron M. Burns.

Route: Pitch 1: From the sandy slope, climb up (5.8) onto a small arch that separates the Ancient Art complex from the formations to the east. Clip an old bolt, and continue up and left to a large ledge. Walk left on the ledge for 50 feet to the base of an obvious chimney. Pitch 2: Climb the obvious chimney (5.10+) to a spacious ledge with two large boulders on it. Pitch 3: Climb down into a cleft behind the ledge, then climb a wild off-width crack/squeeze chimney (5.8) for 40 feet to a spacious ledge. Walk to the right on the ledge, then mantle a small boulder pile and face-climb (5.7) up to a prominent ledge below the summit. Walk left on the ledge to a rappel anchor. Pitch 4: Walk back to the right 20 feet, and mantle onto the summit (5.10+ R).

Special considerations: Pitch 4 is almost totally unprotected. There is no fixed gear on the true summit. Caution is advised. Also, the route can be broken into as many pitches as you deem appropriate for rope drag issues. It was first climbed in six pitches.

Descent: From the summit, it is necessary to down-climb to the top of pitch 3. (Or do a "Duano": Make a huge leap to the lower summit to the southeast.) From the top of pitch 3, make two rappels back to the bench. Down-climb to a small tree, then rappel off it. Or, down-climb the start of the Stolen Chimney route (climb 24).

26 KINGFISHER, COLORADO NORTHEAST RIDGE

First ascent: Harvey Carter and Cleve McCarty, May 27–31, 1962
Difficulty: IV, 5.8, C2
Time: 1–2 days
Equipment: 1 set of wired stoppers; 1 set of Camalots; many tie-offs for bolt studs
Approach: From the Fisher Towers parking lot, follow the Titan Trail to Ancient Art, then hike toward the start of Stolen Chimney. Continue up the major

Climb 26, Kingfisher, Colorado Northeast Ridge. © Cameron M. Burns.

gully between Ancient Art and Cottontail Tower, the huge formation to the south. The Kingfisher is obvious on the left side as you hike up the major gully. It is one of the four biggest towers in the Fisher Towers. The Colorado Northeast Ridge climbs the prominent ridge that forms the uphill edge of the Kingfisher.

Route: Pitch 1: Climb the obvious bolt ladder (C1) to a stance with a fixed anchor. Pitch 2: Ascend a narrow, 5.7 mud chimney above the first stance to a small stance on the crest of the ridge. Pitch 3: Continue up cracks on both free and aid, using camming units and stoppers for aid (5.7, C2). Pitch 4: Climb the overhanging bolt ladder on the northwest side of the ridge, then follow cracks over the caprock

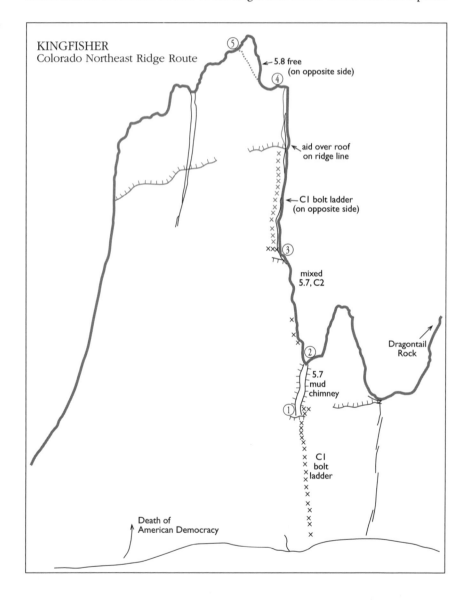

KINGFISHER
Colorado Northeast Ridge Route

← 5.8 free
(on opposite side)

aid over roof
on ridge line

←C1 bolt ladder
(on opposite side)

mixed
5.7, C2

Dragontail
Rock

5.7
mud
chimney

C1
bolt
ladder

Death of
American Democracy

overhang to a large, comfortable belay ledge (5.7, C1). Pitch 5: Climb well-protected cracks and chimneys on the north side of the tower to the summit (5.8).

Special considerations: This route can be broken into any number of pitches, depending on the preference of the climbing party. For example, many parties link pitches 1 and 2 together, and pitch 4 is often done as two pitches, with a hanging belay below the caprock.

Descent: Rappel the route.

27 ECHO TOWER, PHANTOM SPRINT

First ascents: Jim Beyer, February 25–26, 1986. *First clean ascent:* Dougald MacDonald and Dave Goldstein, September 2–3, 1996. *First free ascent:* Stevie Haston, spring 1997.

Difficulty: IV, 5.9, C2+ or III, 5.12

Time: 1–2 days

Equipment: 2 sets of camming units; 2 sets TCUs; 1 set of tri cams; medium hexcentrics; stoppers; a big hook

Approach: From the Fisher Towers parking lot, follow the Titan Trail to Ancient Art, then hike toward the start of Stolen Chimney (climb 24). Continue up the major gully between Ancient Art and Cottontail Tower, the huge formation to the south. The Kingfisher is obvious on the left side as you hike up the major gully. It is one of the four biggest towers in the Fisher Towers. To reach Echo Tower, walk south from the Kingfisher to the next large formation, Echo Tower. (The North Chimney route on Echo Tower climbs the chimney on the tower's north side). Phantom Sprint climbs a crack system on the northeast

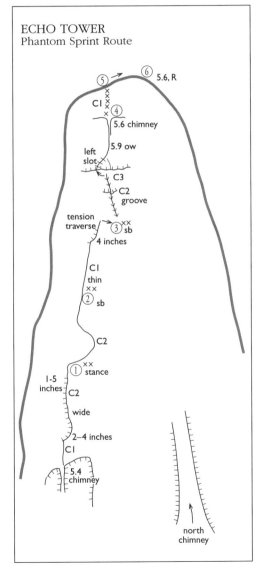

ECHO TOWER
Phantom Sprint Route

face of Echo, up the hill and left of the enormous north chimney, which splits the north face from lower right to upper left. The route starts up a clean, straight-in crack behind a boulder against the base of the face.

Route: Pitch 1: Climb a 5.4 chimney to a large ledge, then continue up a crack and corner (C2) for a full rope length, ending at a stance. Pitch 2: Move up, then right (C2), then back left to a hanging belay. Pitch 3: Climb a C1 crack straight up, then a right-leaning short corner, then tension-traverse right, to a hanging belay. Pitch 4: Continue straight up a C2 groove to a roof, and through a slot on the left (5.9 off-width) into a 5.6 chimney that ends at a ledge at the base of a bolt ladder. Pitch 5: Climb the bolt ladder to the top (C1). Pitch 6: A spectacular hand traverse along the very spine ridge for 30 feet, followed by a mantle and easy climbing to the actual summit pinnacle (5.6, R). Down-climb the pitch to get off.

Special considerations: Pitches 4 and 5 can be done as one pitch. Also, pitch 1 can be broken into two pitches with a belay atop the chimney.

Descent: Make three double-rope rappels down the route.

28 COTTONTAIL TOWER, BRER RABBIT

First ascent: Ed Webster, April 1978

Difficulty: V, 5.9, A3-

Time: 2–3 days

Equipment: 2 sets of wired stoppers with extra medium stoppers; 2 sets of camming units; 2 sets of TCUs or equivalent; a selection of 30 pitons, including Lost Arrows, blades, and angles from ½-inch to 2-inch angles; several Birdbeaks. Sawed-off angles are very helpful; bring a selection.

Approach: From the Fisher Towers parking lot, follow the Titan Trail to Ancient Art, then hike toward the start of Stolen Chimney (climb 24). Continue up the major gully between Ancient Art and Cottontail Tower, the huge formation to the south. At the point where Cottontail Tower juts farthest west is the start of Brer Rabbit, which takes the ridge directly above the trail. Start at the base of the dramatic west ridge, which drops to within 50 feet of the Titan Trail.

Route: Pitches 1–2: Aid up bulges

Luke Laeser starting pitch 6, Brer Rabbit, Cottontail Tower.
© Cameron M. Burns.

Climb 28, Cottontail Tower, Brer Rabbit. © Cameron M. Burns.

and corners straight up the obvious crack system (A2) to a fixed belay. Pitch 3: Move right, around the corner, and free-climb to a big ledge with a roof overhead. Clip a bolt in the roof and mantle it. Pitch 4: Walk left on a huge ledge leading to the north face of the tower. The ledge becomes tilted, but leads to anchors at the base of a thin crack splitting a roof (5.8). Pitch 5: Aid straight up out over the roof (A3-) to a notch with fixed anchors. Pitch 6: Climb the steep off-width above to the large horizontal section of the west ridge (5.9). Pitch 7: Walk along the ridge (jumping across a gap) to the point where it steepens (Class 4). Pitch 8: Aid the old bolt ladder to a thin crack (A2), then stop at the anchors on a ledge. Pitch 9: Traverse right (not straight up!) and climb the back of a large rib on bolts (5.9, A2) to gain the summit ridge and a fixed belay. Pitch 10: Mixed free- and aid-climbing leads up the final ridge to the summit block, which is climbed via a 3-inch crack on the southeast side.

Special considerations: This is one of the hardest routes in this book. Hauling on it is a nightmare.

Climb 28, Cottontail Tower, Brer Rabbit. © Cameron M. Burns.

Descent: From the summit, rappel the route to the top of the long, flat ridge halfway up, near the top of pitch 6. Three sets of bomber rappel anchors—which are almost invisible from the ground—lead down the north face of the landform. Check them out before you begin up the route.

29 TITAN, FINGER OF FATE

First ascent: Layton Kor, George Hurley, and Huntley Ingalls, May 5–6 and 12–13, 1962
Difficulty: IV, 5.9, A2+
Time: 1–2 days
Equipment: 3 sets of wired stoppers with extra medium stoppers (the route sucks up stoppers!); 3 ⅝-inch angles; 3 ¾-inch angles; 2 1-inch angles; 2 sets of Camalots with 1 set of half sizes; 2 0.5 camming units, 2 0.75 camming units

Climb 29, Titan, Finger of Fate. © Cameron M. Burns.

Approach: From the Fisher Towers parking lot, follow the Titan Trail to Ancient Art. To reach the Titan from the Ancient Art area, continue along the Titan Trail for another 0.5 mile or so, passing around the northern, western, and southern edges of Cottontail Tower's base. After leaving Cottontail, the trail dips through another dry wash, then skirts along the northern base of the Titan. To reach the Finger of Fate route, walk right, along the south face of the Titan for about 0.25 mile, then scramble up a steep climbers track leading to the base of the mesa behind the Titan. Gain the shelf connecting the Titan to the wall behind it, and walk toward the Titan. (You actually end up going a few hundred feet away from the Titan to access the shelf that leads to the Finger of Fate route.) The Finger of Fate route should become obvious. It starts on the left side of the northeastern side of the tower, and follows the prominent crack system below a tall gendarme halfway up the Titan (the Finger itself). Start at the bottom of the northeast side of the tower.

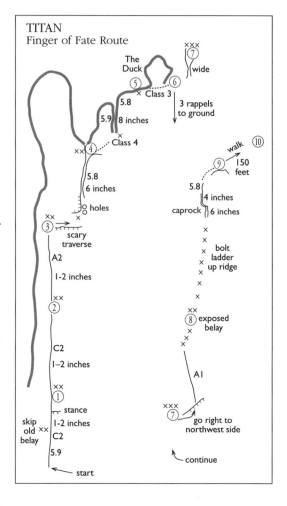

TITAN
Finger of Fate Route

Route: Pitch 1: Free-climb as high as possible (the free-climbing gets progressively harder), then switch to clean aid (C2). Bypass an old sling belay on the left and continue up to a second sling belay on the right, just above a stance (but not on the stance itself), 140 feet off the ground. Pitch 2: Continue up the crack system for 70 feet using aid (C2) and the occasional free move. Pitch 3: Climb on aid (A2) another 70 feet to a ledge just below the base of the Finger, where there is an old bolt belay. Pitch 4: Traverse right 20 feet, around a corner, past some old fixed slings, to gain a small shelf below a crack with a bolt (5.8). Clip the bolt and aid up the crack above it, using whatever works in the holes. Several aid moves lead to free-climbing up an awkward slot (5.8) to a belay. Pitch 5: Continue up and right, past several bolts (C1), then gain the obvious off-width cracks above (5.9) before hitting a one-bolt belay on the crest of the ridge. Pitch 6: Walk for 40 feet along the ridge, past the Duck (the obvious gendarme on the ridge) on its right (northwest), to reach a belay at the top of the Rappel Gully. (From here, it is three double-rope rappels down the gully to the base of the Titan. Many parties climb to this point on their first day, then fix ropes in the gully for their return the following day.) Pitch 7: Climb down and left, and across the small scooped bowl, then up a wide but easy (5.7) cleft for 30 feet to reach a flat belay ledge (the best on the route) and a three-bolt anchor. Pitch 8: Step right, out onto the northwest face, then across a gap to a ledge. Aid up and left in the obvious thin crack, passing several old pitons on the way. The crack reaches the crest of the ridge, passes several more old bolts, and the pitch ends at a wildly exposed belay below the summit ridge. Pitch 9: Climb the ancient bolt ladder up the summit ridge. The cracks through the caprock are wide, and #1, #2, and #4 Camalots are recommended. Finish the pitch with an exposed free move (5.8) onto a ledge with a belay. Pitch 10: Walk along the summit ridge 150 feet to the true summit.

Jesse Harvey following pitch 1, Finger of Fate Route, The Titan, Fisher Towers. © Cameron M. Burns.

Special considerations: Pitches 2 and 3 can be linked together into one lead; however, if you are trying to climb the route as cleanly as possible, you will likely run low on gear by the time you get halfway up pitch 3. Also, pitches 5 and 6 can be done as one pitch, although if you are hauling a bag, the hauling is extremely difficult. Another consideration: Most parties use a few piton stacks in old scars on this route. It is good to familiarize yourself with this technique before beginning up the route. This route has reportedly been done clean, but 99 percent of those who climb it use a handful of pitons.

Descent: Make two double-rope rappels down the route to the top of the Rappel Gully. Then make three more double-rope rappels down the Rappel Gully. There is much loose rock in the Rappel Gully.

30 TITAN, SUNDEVIL CHIMNEY

First ascents: Harvey Carter, Bob Sullivan, Tom Merrill, and Ken Wyrick, April 20–28, 1971. *First clean ascent:* Andy Donson and Kath Pyke, 1999.

Difficulty: VI, 5.9, C4

Time: 2–4 days

Equipment: 2 sets of Friends to #4 Friend; a large selection of stoppers of all sizes; 1 set of Camalots to #5; 3 sets of TCUs or the equivalent; 2 sets of tri cams; a selection of 20 pitons (for placing by hand)

Approach: From the Fisher Towers parking lot, follow the Titan Trail to Ancient Art; continue along the trail for another 0.5 mile or so, passing around the northern, western, and southern edges of Cottontail Tower's base. After leaving Cottontail, the trail dips through another dry wash, then skirts along the northern base of the Titan. Jutting out from the southwestern side of the Titan (the Sundevil Chimney side) is a long shelf, about 100–150 feet high. This shelf, which offers the best access to the Titan, can be climbed near its southwestern end, up an easy ledge system. On the shelf, a trail leads north, directly toward the Titan. The Sundevil Chimney is the obvious vertical cleft splitting the entire tower on its southwestern (and longest) prow. This route follows one continuous crack system from bottom to top.

Route: Pitch 1: Start just right of the Titan's southern prow and move up and to the right into it, using thin cracks and corners. Pitches 2–7: Follow the crack system straight up the cleft.

Special considerations: Pitch 1 is generally considered the crux,

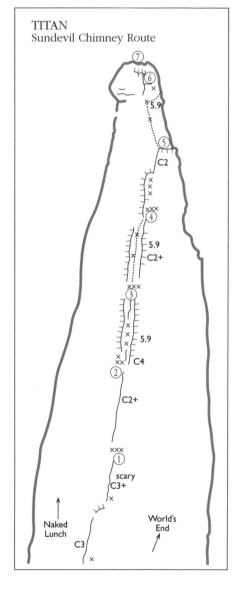

TITAN
Sundevil Chimney Route

5.9

C2

5.9
C2+

5.9

C4

C2+

scary
C3+

Naked
Lunch

World's
End

C3

Climb 30, Titan, Sundevil Chimney. © Cameron M. Burns.

though the first clean ascent team thought the third pitch the crux. Several parties have reportedly worn crampons on this route; supposedly they help. The entire route was recently done clean.

Descent: Rappel this route, or the Finger of Fate route (climb 29).

31 RIVER TOWER, NORTH FACE (A.K.A. THE NORTHWEST CORNER ROUTE)

First ascents: Ken Wyrick and Tom Merrill, November 8–9, 1973.
First solo ascent: Jon Butler, fall 1995.
Difficulty: III, 5.8, C2
Time: 5 hours

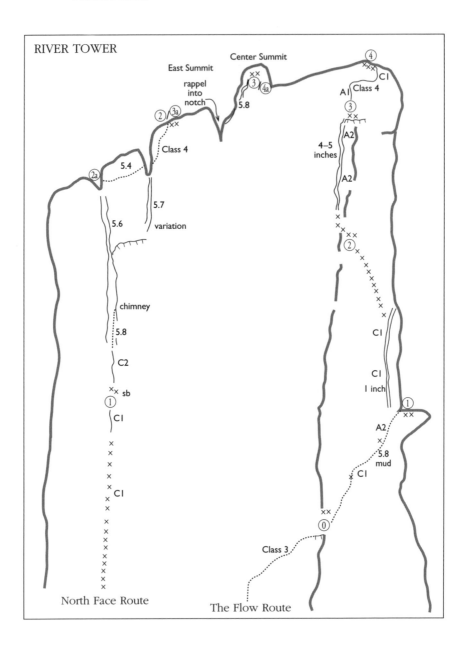

RIVER TOWER

Center Summit

East Summit

rappel into notch

Class 4

5.8

Class 4

A

A2

5.4

5.7

variation

5.6

chimney

5.8

C2

sb

C1

C1

North Face Route

4–5 inches

A2

A2

C1

C1

1 inch

A2

5.8 mud

C1

Class 3

The Flow Route

Equipment: 1 set of camming units; 1 set of TCUs or the equivalent; 3 sets of wired stoppers (mostly to place over bolts with missing hangers); tie-offs

Approach: From the parking spot, walk across several dry washes to near River Tower's base, then scramble up the left or right (north) side of the tower. The North Face route follows a prominent cleft near the left side of the north face. Start at the bottom of the obvious chimney on the north side of the tower, about 150 feet from the tower's east end.

Route: Pitch 1: Aid 150 feet (C1) up the obvious bolt ladder to an uncomfortable hanging belay. Most bolts have no hangers. A few natural gear placements are required just before the belay. Pitch 2: Aid over the roof above the belay, and continue for about 30 feet to a fixed-ring angle piton before free-climbing becomes mandatory. Climb through a wild roof/squeeze chimney (5.8) to reach a big ledge. At this point, it is possible to go two ways: straight up or right. (Pitch 2a: If you continue (Class 4) straight up the main chimney—unprotected 5.6 mud climbing—climb through a broken arch to a huge ledge, then belay. Pitch 3a: Then climb a short traversing pitch west to gain fixed anchors below River Tower's East Summit.) If you go to the right above the roof/squeeze chimney, traverse on a loose but wide ledge to a short crack that leads to the fixed anchors below River Tower's East Summit. The East Summit is an easy scramble above these anchors. Pitch 3 (or 4a): To reach the Center Summit (the Main Summit), fix a rope down into the notch between the East and Main Summits, and rappel into the notch. Then climb a short 5.8 crack to reach the Main Summit. Rappel slings near the summit are obvious.

Descent: From the Main Summit, rappel back into the notch between the Main and East Summits, then climb out of the notch back to the East Summit. (Most parties fix a rope for this return trip and jumar back out of the notch to the East Summit.) Then, from the East Summit anchors, rappel the route.

32 RIVER TOWER, THE FLOW

First ascent: Mike Baker and Cameron Burns, May 1997
Difficulty: III, 5.8, A2
Time: 1 full day
Equipment: 1 set of wired stoppers; 2 ⅝-inch angles; 2 ¾-inch angles; 2 1-inch angles; 2 sets of Camalots with 1 set of half sizes, plus several large sizes for pitch 3

Approach: From the parking spot, walk across several dry washes to near River Tower's base, then scramble up the right (north) side of the tower. The Flow begins at the lower right-hand edge of the tower when viewed from the north. The Flow starts on an exposed ledge with two belay bolts. Start at the base of the northwest side of the landform on the exposed ledge.

Route: Pitch 1: Climb up and right using a mixture of free-climbing and aid, past several bolts to a unique ledge (a large rock sticking sideways out of the southwest corner of the tower) with fixed anchors (5.8, A2). Pitch 2: Climb the crack above the ledge for 30 feet (C1), then move up and left on a bolt ladder to gain a stance and a two-bolt belay. Pitch 3: Move left around the corner on three bolts,

Northwest face of River Tower: climb 31, North Face, and climb 32, The Flow.
© Cameron M. Burns.

then climb the wide crack (4–5 inches) for 80 feet to a fixed belay in the band of caprock (5.8, A2). Pitch 4: Climb up and left for 10 feet (A1), then move right on a large ledge (Class 4) and climb two short walls (C1) to reach the top of the tower and fixed anchors.

Special considerations: If it has not been done already, the route will likely be done clean in the near future.

Descent: Make three double-rope rappels down the west face from fixed anchors at the summit, atop pitch 2, and atop pitch 1.

ARCHES NATIONAL PARK

Arches National Park is a magical place, boasting not only the largest concentration of natural stone arches in the world (over 2,000 have been catalogued), but also a tremendous number of beautiful rock towers, fins, and buttes.

The wild formations found in Arches are the result of massive geologic forces. Three hundred million years ago, an inland sea covered the Colorado Plateau and as it evaporated, it deposited billions of tons of salt. As erosion continued, other depositions came and went. The salt layer buckled and shifted, dissolved and moved, causing massive uplift in some places and massive depression in others. In Arches, you can almost see geologic forces at work.

Added to the fact that most of the park sits upon several high mesas offering beautiful views of the La Sal mountains and Castle Valley to the east, it's not surprising that it's a popular place for visitors.

Arches' appeal to climbers is due both to the park's beauty and the ease of access to most of the routes found here. And despite Arches' compact size, rock climbs within the park vary wildly from easy one-pitch, free routes to difficult 600-foot, multipitch aid affairs. The routes in this chapter are a sampling of some of the park's best.

Area climbing regulations: Climbers should check at the visitor center for the current status of climbing in the park. Certain formations can be closed for nesting raptors. Arches National Park does allow the use of pitons and the placement of bolts; however, the park service asks climbers not to place fixed gear unless an existing anchor is deemed unsafe. Motorized drills and white chalk are prohibited.

Special considerations: The rock in Arches is extremely soft Entrada sandstone, hence clean climbing practices are very much encouraged. Also, with a vast number of tourists sitting below many of the climbing routes, climbers should be on their best behavior here.

Getting there: Arches National Park lies just 5 miles north of Moab, Utah, on US 191. From Moab, drive north on US 191, cross the Colorado River, then continue north for 2.8 miles to the park entrance on the right. From I-70, take exit 180, onto US 191 south, and drive 27 miles to the park entrance.

After driving a few hundreds yards along the park's main road, the visitor center is to the right. From the visitor center, drive through the park for 4 miles to reach a large parking lot on the right, at the Courthouse Towers Viewpoint. This parking lot, below the west face of The Organ, is a good place to park for routes on Argon Tower, the Three Gossips, The Organ, and Tower of Babel.

To reach Off-Balanced Rock and Owl Rock, continue past the Courthouse Towers parking lot to the turnoff to the Windows Section of the park, 9.9 miles past the visitor center. Turn right (east); Off-Balanced Rock is immediately on your right. It is the first formation south of the intersection. From the intersection, continue southeast on the Windows Section road approximately 1 mile to the Garden of Eden parking area on your left. Park here to reach Owl Rock, the obvious rounded tower just 100 feet to the east.

To reach Dark Angel, from the intersection of the park's main road and the

Windows Section road, continue to drive on the park's main road all the way through the park, roughly 18 miles from the visitor center, to the end of the park road; park in the Devil's Garden parking lot, which can get quite full. The hike to the tower starts here.

33 ARGON TOWER, WEST FACE

First ascents: Steve Cheyney and John Pease, Spring 1972. *First solo ascent:* Luke Laeser, 1994.
Difficulty: II, 5.11 or 5.9+, C1
Time: ½ day
Equipment: 2 sets of Camalots up to #4 size with extra #2 and #3; 2 sets of TCUs; 2 sets of stoppers

Approach: From the Courthouse Towers Viewpoint parking lot, Argon Tower is the most slender, fingerlike spire across the road (south) of the parking lot. It is a

Pitch 1, West Face, Argon Tower, Arches National Park. © Cameron M. Burns.

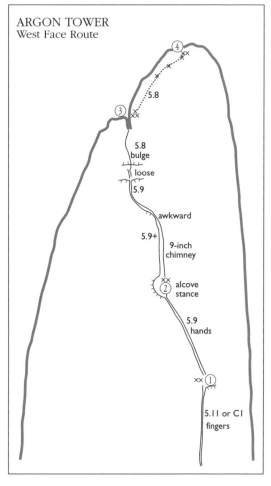

ARGON TOWER
West Face Route

④
5.8
③
5.8 bulge
loose
5.9
awkward
5.9+
9-inch chimney
② alcove stance
5.9 hands
①
5.11 or C1 fingers

short hike to its base. The West Face route climbs the prominent crack system on the far southern end of the west face.

Route: Pitch 1: Climb a thin but widening crack to a ledge (5.11 or C1). Pitch 2: Climb the hand crack above the ledge (5.9) to a cramped alcove stance in a chimney. Pitch 3: Squeeze up the slot above (5.9+), then go over several small bulges (5.9) and belay at a ledge on the north ridge. Pitch 4: Face-climb past two bolts to the summit (5.8).

Descent: Rappel the route.

34 THREE GOSSIPS, SPEAK NO EVIL

First ascent: Duane and Lisa Raleigh, winter 1994. *First-pitch variation:* Jeff Widen and Jon Plvan, fall 1994.

Difficulty: III, 5.10, C2

Time: 1 full day

Equipment: 2 sets of Camalots up to #5 size; 2 sets of TCUs; 2 sets of Lowe Balls

Approach: From the Courthouse Towers Viewpoint parking lot, the Three Gossips is the three-summitted butte across the road and west of Argon Tower. It is a short hike to its base. If one divides the east face of the tower into two walls, separated by the three "heads" of the formation, Speak No Evil climbs the prominent crack system halfway between the north (right) head and the middle head. It starts by going around a pointed roof.

Route: Pitch 1: Follow the thin (½-inch) splitter crack, which widens to 4 inches, for a full rope length to a one-bolt stance (5.10, C1). The Widen-Plvan Variation to the first pitch is highly recommended. It starts 30 feet left of the normal start,

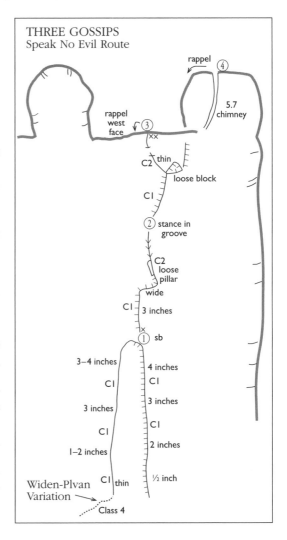

THREE GOSSIPS
Speak No Evil Route

Above: *Three Gossips, Speak No Evil, showing the original start (climb 34) and the Widen-Plvan Variation (34a).* © Cameron M. Burns. Right: *John Plvan on pitch 2, Speak No Evil, Three Gossips, Arches National Park, 1994.* © Jeff Widen.

and follows a splitter hand crack (C1) to the first belay. Pitch 2: Nut out the overhanging black rock 65 feet to a stance in a groove (C2). Pitch 3: Move up and left (C2) to the ridge between the two Gossips. Pitch 4: Join the West Face Route (climb 35) to the summit: worm up the chimney (5.7).

Special considerations: The Widen-Plvan Variation will likely go free.

Descent: Rappel the West Face Route (climb 35).

35 THREE GOSSIPS, WEST FACE ROUTE

First ascent: Allen Steck and Steve Roper, October 1970. *First free ascent:* Glen Randall and Jeff Achey, 1982.

Difficulty: III, 5.11 or 5.9, C1

Climb 35, Three Gossips, West Face Route. © Cameron M. Burns.

Time: 5 hours

Equipment: 2 sets of wired stoppers; 2 sets of Camalots with extra #2–#3 and a #5 size

Approach: From the Courthouse Towers Viewpoint parking lot, the Three Gossips is the three-summitted butte across the road and west of Argon Tower. It is a short hike to its base. The West Face Route lies around the corner to the right (counterclockwise), on the west face. It climbs the continuous crack system below and right of the north "head."

Route: Pitch 1: Mantle some loose ledges (5.9) and climb 110 feet up a stunning hand crack in a corner to a ledge with fixed anchors. Pitch 2: Continue up the same crack system. The climbing gets progressively harder (to 5.11 or C1). Belay on a ledge below the summit block. Pitch 3: Worm up the chimney (5.7) above to the summit.

Descent: Rappel the route.

36 THE ORGAN, THELMA AND LOUISE

First ascent: Stevie Haston and Laurence Gouault, April 1994. This route is a variation of Death by Hands, first climbed by Peter Gallagher and Steve Sommers, March 1986.

Difficulty: IV, 5.11+

Time: 1 full day

Equipment: 2 sets of wired stoppers; 2 sets of Camalots with #5 size; TCUs

Approach: The Organ (a twin-summitted butte) lies just east of the Courthouse Towers Viewpoint parking lot, essentially towering above the parking lot. Thelma

The west face of The Organ: climb 36, Thelma and Louise; climb 37, Dune.
© Cameron M. Burns.

and Louise climbs a crack system located on the northern edge of the southwestern tower, near the large cleft separating the two towers.

Route: Pitch 1: Climb a long (180 feet), difficult-to-protect slab pitch (5.9 R) up shallow ramps and minor cracks to the base of the headwall, and belay. Pitch 2: Climb the widening crack above, past an old bolt, to a decent belay stance (5.11+). Pitch 3: Continue up the corner above (5.10) to a belay on top of a pillar. Pitch 4: Climb the right side of broken blocks to a belay with fixed anchors. Pitch 5: Walk through a tunnel and climb a short pitch to the crest of the summit ridge (5.10+). Pitch 6: Climb Class 4 to the summit.

Special considerations: On this route, 200-foot ropes are helpful.

Descent: Make four double-rope rappels into the cleft between the southwestern and northeastern towers of The Organ.

37 THE ORGAN, DUNE

First ascent: Duane Raleigh, April 1986
Difficulty: IV, 5.10+, C3-
Time: 1–2 days
Equipment: 2 sets of wired stoppers; 4 sets of Camalots with #5 size; 2 sets of TCUs

Approach: The Organ (a twin-summitted butte) lies just east of the Courthouse Towers Viewpoint parking lot, essentially towering above the parking lot. Dune climbs the prominent buttress that lies above the northern end of the parking lot.

Route: Pitch 1: Climb the right-facing corner directly below the west buttress of The Organ to a ledge above the corner (5.10, C1). Pitch 2: Climb a sandy groove to fixed anchors at the base of a large, steep corner system (5.7). Pitch 3: Climb the awesome corner/crack system above the belay to a hanging belay (5.10, C2). Pitch 4: Continue up the corner (5.10 or C1) to an easy chimney, then move right, on ledges, to the base of a splitter crack piercing the upper headwall of the tower. Pitch 5: Climb up the splitter (C2+/C3-), then scramble to the top.

Special considerations: The route reportedly goes clean. The six or so pitons placed by Raleigh on the first ascent were used only because he carried no TCUs. One might find a couple of pins handy for the last pitch, which gets dirty. Also, it's possible to skip the first pitch by traversing in from far to the left, after doing the first pitch of Death by Hands (see Thelma and Louise, climb 36).

Descent: Make four double-rope rappels into the cleft between the southwestern and northeastern towers of The Organ.

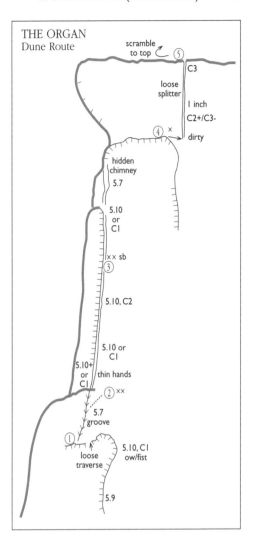

THE ORGAN
Dune Route

scramble to top ⑤
C3
loose splitter
1 inch
C2+/C3-
④ × dirty
hidden chimney
5.7
5.10 or C1
×× sb ③
5.10, C2
5.10 or C1
5.10+ or C1 / thin hands
② ××
5.7 groove
①
loose traverse
5.10, C1 ow/fist
5.9

38 TOWER OF BABEL, ZENYATTA ENTRADA

First ascents: Charlie Fowler, Eric Bjørnstad, and Lin Ottinger, October 1986. *First solo ascent:* Linus Platt, 1990.
Difficulty: IV, 5.8, C3
Time: 1–2 days
Equipment: 3 sets of wired stoppers; 2 sets of Camalots; 3 sets of TCUs; Lowe Balls; a selection of hooks
Approach: The Tower of Babel lies just west of the Courthouse Towers Viewpoint parking lot. The Zenyatta Entrada route follows the thin crack system on the southern end of the tower. Begin on the right side of the face. The route follows the lone crack system splitting the south end of the butte for six pitches.

Climb 38, Tower of Babel, Zenyatta Entrada. © Cameron M. Burns.

Route: Pitch 1: Climb cracks just left of the large flake pedestal at the base of the tower to gain a small ledge 115 feet off the ground (C2). Pitch 2: Climb a left-facing corner to a ledge (C1), 85 feet. Pitch 3: Climb a crack to a pendulum left to a 1½-inch crack in a flake system that arches up and right, to a good ledge (C2+), 140 feet. Pitch 4: Climb a steep, left-facing corner over a roof to a "bolt" ladder, 75 feet (see Special Considerations, below). Pitch 5: More "bolts" lead to a right-facing flake and the southeast shoulder (C3), 80 feet. Walk to the right to reset the belay below the next lead. Pitch 6: Bolts lead to the summit (5.8, C1), 40 feet.

Special considerations: This route has been done completely clean, but early nailing ascents of this route have caused huge plates of the varnished rock to break off. This prompts some climbers to want to renail. Please don't.

Also, the first ascent party cleaned many fixed bolts (drilled angles). These have been sporadically replaced, but some holes may still exist. If you repeat the route and replace missing fixed gear, please leave it in place. The replacement and removal of drilled angles not only make the route harder (by increasing the size of the subsequent hole) but make some awful scars. Also, the cruxes of the pitches have historically been hook moves in the empty holes. Once all these bolts are replaced, it will likely be a much easier climb.

Finally, on several pitches, it is wise to leave a rope fixed to allow you to pull yourself into rappel stations.

Descent: Rappel the route.

39 OFF-BALANCED ROCK, NORTHEAST CHIMNEY

First ascent: Unknown
Difficulty: I, 5.7
Time: 1 hour
Equipment: 2 sets of camming units, with a selection of small technical Friends or ½ and ¾ size units

Climb 39, Off-Balanced Rock, Northeast Chimney. © Cameron M. Burns.

Approach: From the turnoff to the Windows Section of the park, 9.9 miles past the visitor center, Off-Balanced Rock is immediately on your right. It is the first formation south of the intersection. The tower is a short walk from the road. Start at the bottom of the north side of the tower.

Route: Pitch 1: Climb up the obvious crack/chimney system (5.6) that moves up and right, to a small stance (no fixed anchors) below an off-width. Pitch 2: Climb the off-width above (5.7) for 25 feet, pass a fixed piton, then move to the right for 50 feet into the very middle of the chimney splitting the tower. Climb the chimney using the crack system on the south side of the chimney for protection. The crack

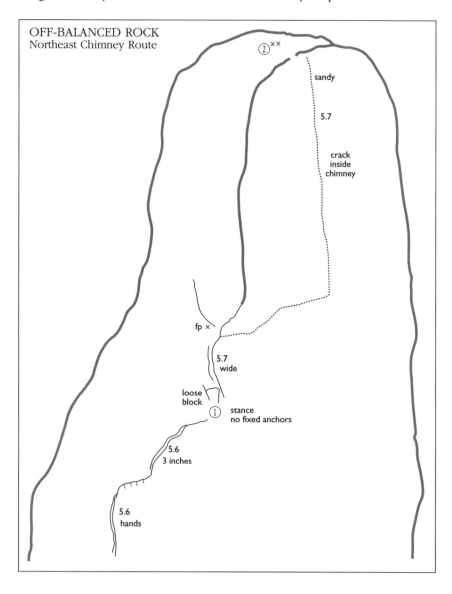

OFF-BALANCED ROCK
Northeast Chimney Route

sandy

5.7

crack
inside
chimney

fp ×

5.7
wide

loose
block

stance
no fixed anchors

5.6
3 inches

5.6
hands

varies in width, and the protection is excellent. The pitch ends at two bolts just below the summit.

Special considerations: It is illegal to climb Balanced Rock, which lies a few hundred feet south of Off-Balanced Rock.

Descent: Make one double-rope rappel down the route.

40 OWL ROCK, OLEVSKY ROUTE

First ascent: Ron Olevsky, February 1978
Difficulty: I, 5.8
Time: ½ hour
Equipment: 1 set of wired stoppers; 1 set of camming units; 10 quickdraws

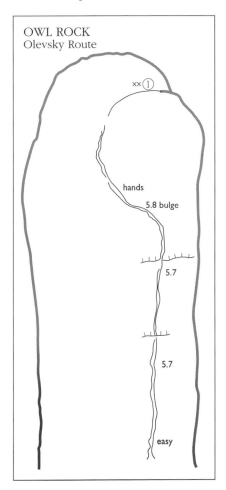

Climb 40, Owl Rock, Olevsky Route.
© Cameron M. Burns.

Approach: From the Garden of Eden parking area, Owl Rock is the obvious rounded tower just 100 feet to the east. Start at the bottom of the west side of the tower.

Route: Pitch 1: Climb up the obvious crack/chimney system to two bolts just below the summit. Scramble to the top.

Special considerations: The route takes hexcentric nuts better than Friends; however, Friends will work.

Descent: Make one double-rope rappel down the west face from fixed anchors on the summit.

41 DARK ANGEL, WEST FACE

First ascent: Dave Rearick and Bob Kamps, November 29, 1962

Difficulty: I, 5.10+/11- or
I, 5.9+, C1

Time: 2 hours

Equipment: 1 set of wired stoppers; several medium camming units; 12 quickdraws

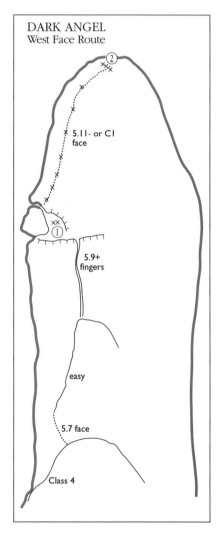

DARK ANGEL
West Face Route

5.11- or C1
face

5.9+
fingers

easy

5.7 face

Class 4

Approach: From the Devil's Garden parking lot, follow the Double O Arch trail north out of the parking lot for roughly 3 miles. The trail twists and turns through slot canyons and over sandstone ridges before reaching Double O Arch. From Double O Arch, Dark Angel is visible roughly 0.5 mile to the north. Follow the obvious trail that leads northwest to the tower. Start at the bottom of the northwest side of the tower.

Route: Pitch 1: Climb up a loose ramp that leads from left (north) to right, and gains an obvious finger crack at the center of the west face of the tower. Climb the finger crack (5.9+), then step left onto a ledge and belay at fixed anchors. Pitch 2: Mantle the block left of the belay and climb past about 10 bolts to the summit (5.10+/11- or C1).

Special considerations: The route can be done in one pitch, though rope drag is bad.

Descent: Make one double-rope rappel down the west face.

CANYONLANDS NATIONAL PARK

Canyonlands National Park is one of the grandest national parks in the Southwest. With its wide, sweeping canyons and huge open basins, portions of the park can be more reminiscent of the surface of the moon than many places on Mother Earth.

The superb Wingate sandstone, which constitutes the upper half of most of Canyonlands, and the fantastic otherworldly scenery of Monument Basin offer the climber a truly extraordinary climbing experience, although recent park regulations have basically stopped new routes from being put up in Canyonlands.

Historically, many of the more prominent towers in Canyonlands were climbed using some kind of aid, and the prevailing impression to many visiting climbers (who read "A" ratings in the old guidebooks) is that those towers are now off-limits because of Canyonlands' strict, "no-piton" regulations. In reality, most of the routes in this chapter were either done on clean aid to begin with, or have been done on clean aid since Canyonlands' strict regulations were created in 1994. Only two towers in this guide, Chip and Dale Towers (climbs 46 and 47), have not yet had clean ascents, and it's just a matter of time before they do. Aid-climbing is anything but a crime in today's Canyonlands; just think clean thoughts and you'll get up any route in this book.

There are two main climbing areas within Canyonlands: Taylor Canyon, home to Moses, Zeus, and other godly towers, and the White Rim Road, where you'll find Monster Tower, Washer Woman, and other Wingate sandstone towers, and the crumbling Cutler sandstone towers of Monument Basin. Also included is a third area, Shafer Canyon, far less well-known, but with a unique approach and excellent climbing in a remote setting.

Area climbing regulations: In the mid-1990s, Canyonlands National Park became the most restrictive park for climbing in the desert southwest, when new fixed anchors were banned. Pitons, bolts, fixed stoppers or camming units, and even rappel slings (all considered fixed anchors) in new locations are banned, which essentially limits climbing within the park to existing routes. Existing anchors should only be replaced if they are deemed unsafe. Motorized drills are prohibited. Climbers should check the current status of climbing in the park at the Island in the Sky Visitor Center. Certain formations can be closed for nesting raptors.

Because approaching many of the routes in Canyonlands requires a healthy afternoon's worth of driving, many climbers choose to camp before a climb. Camping permits are required and camping is limited in Canyonlands, hence the established campgrounds are booked often years in advance. The best way to camp legally in Canyonlands is to get a backcountry camping permit, available at the Island in the Sky Visitor Center.

Special considerations: All these routes in Canyonlands are serious, backcountry, high-commitment affairs, not only in a climbing sense, but also in a "getting yourself and a vehicle in and out" sense. Be prepared. Also, before climbing towers along the White Rim Road, a drive along the Island in the Sky mesa can be helpful. At the Buck Canyon Overlook, one can see the Washer Woman/Monster Tower/Tiki Tower/Airport Tower area to the north, and from the Grand View Point overlook, about 12 miles south of the visitor center along the Island in the Sky Road, one can get a decent view of Monument Basin.

Getting to Taylor Canyon: From Moab, drive north on US 191 to its intersection with Hwy. 313, 9.1 miles north of Hwy. 128 (River Road). Turn left (west) and follow Hwy. 313 for approximately 12 miles. Turn right, onto Horsethief Trail, and follow it for a dozen miles or so out across the mesa. The road reaches the mesa edge, then drops dramatically down a series of switchbacks. Two-wheel drives are okay down the switchbacks. At the bottom of the canyon, turn left and drive 4.3 miles to the boundary of Canyonlands National Park. Look for Charlie Horse Needle, 1.2 miles past (south of) the park boundary on the hillside to the left (seeing it requires a little bit of driving and looking, as the view of it from the road is blocked by low cliffs). Park wherever possible.

To reach Moses and Zeus, continue on another 1.2 miles past Charlie Horse Needle to a fork in the road. Take the left fork (Taylor Canyon Road), and follow it 5.4 miles to its end, where there is a small parking lot for Moses tower. The last 3 miles or so are pretty rough, and four-wheel drive is recommended.

Getting to White Rim Road: Towers along the White Rim area of Canyonlands (Chip and Dale Towers, Washer Woman, Monster Tower, etc.) and towers in Monument Basin (Standing Rock, Shark's Fin, etc.) can be reached by two different routes: the Shafer Trail and Potash Road (a.k.a. Wall Street).

To get there via the Shafer Trail, from Moab, drive north on US 191 to its intersection with Hwy. 313, 9.1 miles north of Hwy. 128 (River Road). Turn left (west) and follow Hwy. 313 toward the Island in the Sky area. After entering the park, but before reaching the visitor center, at 19.5 miles the Shafer Trail is on the left (east). Turn down it and drive for 3 miles to the switchbacks. If the road is wet or snowy, traveling down the Shafer Trail is impossible. Follow the Shafer Trail to the bottom of the canyon, where it meets the Potash Road, which comes in from the left. To reach towers along the White Rim Road, continue straight (southeast).

To use the Potash Road approach, from Moab drive north on US 191, cross the Colorado River, then turn left on Potash Road. (This intersection is a good place to zero out your odometer.) Follow Potash Road past the popular Wall Street climbing area. At about 16.5 miles, the Potash Road veers left around a railroad facility and becomes a dirt road. It then becomes much windier, climbing in and out of canyons and over the railroad tracks. At 25.2 miles, the road goes through a gate with the insignia "TK." (Leave the gate as you find it.) At 30 miles, Potash Road enters Canyonlands National Park. At 31.9 miles, the Potash Road meets the Shafer Trail coming down from the Island in the Sky area of Canyonlands. Turn left onto the Shafer Trail, which becomes the White Rim Road.

Chip and Dale Towers are located roughly 4 miles from the Shafer Trail/Potash Road intersection via an easy scramble from the White Rim Road. Tiki Tower is in the general Airport Tower/Washer Woman/Monster Tower area. It is a thin, flat-topped tower that sits at the northwestern end of a long, broken-up butte of light-colored rock that is on the same ridge as Airport Tower. To reach Tiki Tower, drive roughly 15 miles from the Potash Road/Shafer Trail intersection to the northern side of the subsidiary canyon housing Monster Tower and Washer Woman, and park. (I recommend continuing 0.7 mile to the parking spot for Washer Woman and Monster Tower, so you can get a decent view of Tiki Tower to the north, and from there figure out the approach, a massive hike north up gullies and benches toward the tower.) Parking for Monster Tower and Washer Woman is roughly 15.7 miles from the Shafer Trail/Potash Road intersection. Although there are few distinguishing landmarks, it is best to park where the road crosses a small wash and the towers become obvious on the hillside above. Blocktop and Islet in the Sky are located a couple of miles south of Monster Tower and Washer Woman and should be obvious from the latter. To reach them, continue south along the road until you can hike toward them.

To reach Monument Basin (where Standing Rock and Shark's Fin are located), continue south on the White Rim Road until the basin comes into view below the bench that the road is on. It's roughly 30 miles to Monument Basin from the Shafer Trail/Potash Road intersection. Most climbers gauge the drive in time: about 3 hours. There are numerous places where one can rappel into the basin (leaving ropes fixed for the return to the rim). There is also a place where one can scramble down. The recommended approach is on the north side of Monument Basin (the side you first get to in driving there on the White Rim Road), where there is a thin peninsula of land that juts out on the eastern side of the basin. On the southwest side of this peninsula, an old shepherd's trail (it may require some hunting around to find) leads down into the basin. From the south side of the basin, where a similar peninsula of land juts north into the basin, on the east side of this peninsula (near a car turnaround area), it's possible to scramble down.

Getting to Shafer Canyon: One of the finest, more accessible (at least in terms of distance from Moab) areas for climbing in Canyonlands is on its northeast side, in Shafer Canyon, a spur of deep canyon that juts northwest between the Island in the Sky mesa and Dead Horse Point, a promontory of land jutting east from Island in the Sky. Two fine towers are found here: the twin-summitted Crow's Head Spires and Bird's Eye Butte. Getting to these two towers is best done by rappelling into the canyon, and leaving ropes fixed for the return to the canyon rim.

Before rapping in, it's a good idea to check out the towers' location and access from the road. One good place is along Hwy. 313 (the road between US 191 and Island in the Sky) at a point just inside the park boundary a few miles south of the Dead Horse Point Road. Park at the huge Canyonlands National Park sign and hike directly east, to the canyon edge. The Crow's Head Spires and Bird's Eye Butte are obvious below. There is a possible descent here, at a point where the cliffs are broken and shorter than in other places. Finding it requires hunting around a bit. Directly across the canyon to the east is Dead Horse Point, another point from which the spires can be examined. (Hike down behind the campground when you get to Dead Horse Point State Park.)

The most common rappel point, however, is located directly north of the Crow's Head Spires, on a promontory of land jutting toward the spires. Getting there requires a straightforward drive from the main Island in the Sky Road. From the intersection of Hwy. 313 (which leads to Dead Horse Point) and the Island in the Sky

Road, drive south along the Island in the Sky Road for exactly 1.3 miles and turn left onto an unmarked, barely used dirt road. Follow it east for 0.2 mile, passing an old corral on the right. Exactly 2 miles from the Island in the Sky Road (1.8 miles past the corral) is a road heading southeast (right). Turn here, and follow this dirt road for exactly 2.1 miles. The road becomes rougher and rougher as it reaches the promontory overlooking the Crow's Head Spires. There's a parking spot near the canyon edge.

TAYLOR CANYON AREA

42 CHARLIE HORSE NEEDLE, NORTH FACE

First ascents: Ron Olevsky and Joy Ungritch, May 1985. *First free ascent:* Ken Simms, Mark Hesse, and Maura Hanning, 1995.
Difficulty: III, 5.11c or 5.7, C2
Time: 1 full day
Equipment: 2 sets of Friends; 1 set of TCUs; 2 #5 Camalots; 2 sets of stoppers

Approach: From the parking spot at 4.3 miles on Horsethief Trail, negotiate your way 1.2 miles past (south of) the park boundary to Charlie Horse Needle, on the hillside to the left. To reach the base of the tower from below its north side, hike up and left (east) to gain the bench that runs along the base of the north face. The North Face route climbs the obvious top-to-bottom cleft that splits the tower.

Route: Pitch 1: Climb an off-width, then a chimney to a natural gear belay on a sloping ledge (5.9+ or 5.7, C1). Pitch 2: Continue up the crack system to a fixed anchor on a ledge (5.10 or 5.7, C2). Pitch 3: Climb the thin crack to the summit ridge (5.11c or 5.7, C2) and fixed anchors. Pitch 4: Scramble to the true summit (5.6).

Special considerations: There are several variations.

Descent: Down-climb from the summit to the top of pitch 3, then rappel the route.

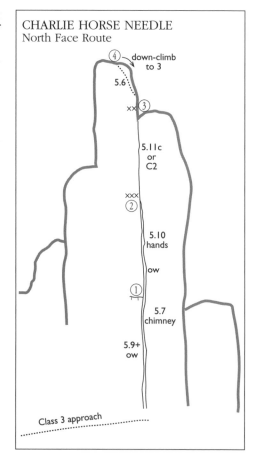

CHARLIE HORSE NEEDLE
North Face Route

④ down-climb to 3
5.6

xx ③

5.11c
or
C2

xxx
②

5.10
hands

ow

①

5.7
chimney

5.9+
ow

Class 3 approach

43 MOSES, PRIMROSE DIHEDRALS

First ascents: Ed Webster, April 19–20, 1979. *First free ascent:* Ed Webster and Steve Hong, October 1979.

Difficulty: IV, 5.10, C1 or 5.11+

Time: 1 full day

Equipment: 2 sets of camming units; 1 set of TCUs; 1 set of wired stoppers

Approach: From the parking point at the end of Taylor Canyon Road, hike east toward the southeast side of the tower. Primrose Dihedrals is the prominent crack system on the right (east) side of the south face. Primrose Dihedrals starts near the junction of Moses and Zeus (the next tower to the east).

Route: Pitch 1: Chimney up the obvious, inverted slot (5.11+ or C1) and continue up easier ground to a bolted belay. Pitch 2: Traverse left, past a bolt under a

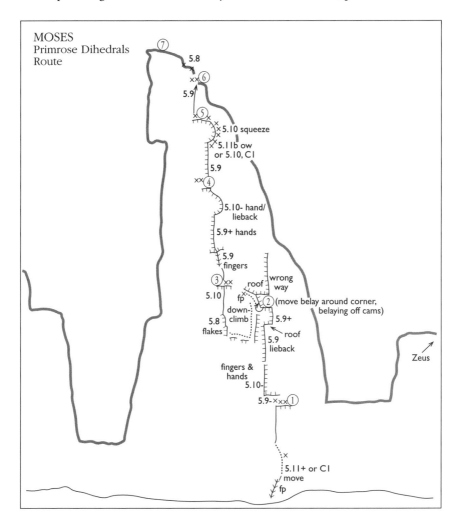

MOSES
Primrose Dihedrals
Route

⑦
5.8
xx ⑥
5.9
⑤
x 5.10 squeeze
x 5.11b ow
or 5.10, C1
5.9
xx ④
5.10- hand/
lieback
5.9+ hands
5.9 fingers
③ xx
roof
wrong way
5.10
fp
down-
climb
② (move belay around corner, belaying off cams)
5.8
flakes
5.9+
5.9 roof
5.9
lieback
Zeus
fingers & hands
5.10-
5.9- xx ①
5.11+ or C1
move
fp

Climb 43, Moses, Primrose Dihedrals.
© Cameron M. Burns.

roof to a left-facing dihedral. Climb the dihedral to its top, then a right-facing dihedral above. Mount a small roof, above which are more roofs. Move left around the corner and belay below a large roof (5.9+) on camming units. Pitch 3: Climb a left-facing dihedral to the base of a large roof, then, bypassing some fixed gear, down-climb the route 10 feet past the belay until it is possible to move left on flakes that lead up again. Climb a 5.10 crack to a large belay ledge directly across from the roof. Pitch 4: Climb a superb right-facing dihedral past an over-hanging flake to a sloping belay ledge with fixed anchors. Pitch 5: Continue up a broken right-facing dihedral to an off-width, the "Ear." Climb the off-width (5.11b) to a squeeze chimney and a good belay ledge. Pitch 6: Move up and right via face-climbing and cracks to the junction of the northeast ridge and the Pale Fire Route. Pitch 7: Face-climb up the ridge to the summit.

Special considerations: The pitches are all short and some can be linked together. A variation to the first pitch traverses from the notch east of the tower into the first belay (5.8). Also, twin-rope technique helps on pitch 3. Most parties yard up the bolts around the Ear on pitch 5 (C1).

Descent: Rappel the route or, if it's crowded, rappel Diretissima, the route left of Primrose Dihedrals. It's a good idea to scope Diretissima from the ground before you start climbing.

44 MOSES, DUNN ROUTE

First ascents: Jimmy Dunn, Doug Snively, Stewart Green, and Kurt Rasmussen, 1973. *First free ascent:* Jeff Achey and Glenn Randall, 1982.
Difficulty: IV, 5.11
Time: 1 full day

Equipment: 2 sets of camming units up to #5 Camalot; 1 set of TCUs; 1 set of wired stoppers

Approach: From the parking point at the end of Taylor Canyon Road, hike east toward the north side of the tower. The Dunn Route climbs a corner system on the right side of the north face.

Route: Pitch 1: Scramble up broken ledges to a right-facing corner/off-width crack and climb it to a sling belay (5.9+). Pitch 2: Continue up the corner above the belay, pass a bolt, then either go left in a broken crack system (5.9) or right, into a steep chimney (5.9). Belay at a ledge on the crest of the west ridge. Pitch 3: Move left to a big ledge and a belay below an overhanging hand crack (5.9+). Pitch 4: Climb the hand crack (5.11 or C1) until it widens, then squeeze inside the chimney and work over to Moses's left "shoulder" and fixed anchors. Pitch 5: Climb a 5.8 face to the summit.

Special considerations: Also known as the Dunn-Snively Route. Pitch 2's left variation requires a 200-foot or longer rope.

Descent: Rappel the route to the left, Pale Fire, or rappel Diretissima on the south face.

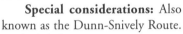

Jeff Widen on pitch 4, Primrose Dihedrals, Moses, Canyonlands National Park. Photo: Tony Valdes/Widen collection.

45 ZEUS, SISYPHUS

First ascents: Jimmy Dunn and Doug Snively, 1973. *First free ascent:* Chip Chace and Jeff Achey, 1981.

Difficulty: III, 5.11+ R

Time: 1 full day

Equipment: 2 sets of Friends to #3 with an extra #1; 1 #3.5 and #4 Friends; 2 sets of TCUs; 1 set of stoppers

Approach: From the parking lot at the end of Taylor Canyon Road, hike east. Zeus is the obvious slender spire sitting on the same ridge as Moses, but lying a few hundred yards to its east. Sisyphus climbs the obvious dihedral system on the left side of Zeus's south face.

Climb 45, Zeus, Sisyphus. © Cameron M. Burns.

Route: Pitch 1: Begin up a right-facing corner past the "pod" to a mantle, then a thin crack in a corner to a decent ledge with no fixed anchors (5.11-). Pitch 2: Continue up the corner system (5.11), with the climbing getting progressively easier, to a 5.8 chimney. Exit the chimney and move right, up stacked blocks, then back left slightly to a belay at fixed anchors. Pitch 3: Climb the thin corner above the belay, then move right, on a ledge, to a steep, thin move over a bulge (5.11+) with poor protection. Scramble up and right, to the summit.

Special considerations: This is a hard free route with a scary third pitch.

Descent: Rappel the low-angled East Ridge, past dozens of chopped bolts.

WHITE RIM ROAD

46 DALE TOWER, BOYS' NIGHT OUT

First ascent: Jeff Widen, Cameron Burns, and Jeff Singer, October 2, 1994
Difficulty: III, 5.9, C1
Time: 6 hours
Equipment: 2 sets of camming units to #5; 2 sets of TCUs; stoppers; a couple of large hooks might help on pitch 3

Approach: Dale Tower, taller than its twin, Chip Tower, is an easy scramble from the White Rim Road. The route ascends the north face of the tower, starting in a crack system below a long chimney that leads to a notch just right of the summit tower.

Route: Pitch 1: Climb thin cracks over a roof (5.9, C1), then the chimney

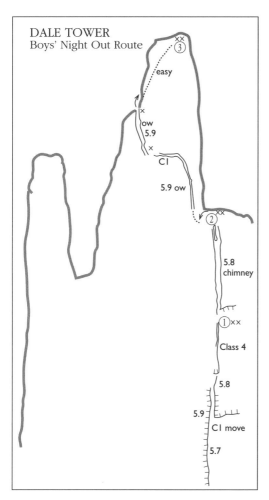

Jeff Singer on pitch 2, Boys' Night Out, Dale Tower, Canyonlands National Park. © Cameron M. Burns.

Climb 46, Dale Tower, Boys' Night Out. © Cameron M. Burns.

above (5.8) to a stance with fixed anchors. Pitch 2: Continue up the chimney to the ridge (5.8). Pitch 3: Down-climb through a notch to an off-width, then climb it to its top (5.9). Move left using an edge (C1) to gain another off-width leading to the summit.

Special considerations: The first ascent party used only a few pitons. Subsequent ascents will undoubtedly go clean, and free.

Descent: Rappel the route.

47 CHIP TOWER, STUFFIN' NUTS

First ascent: Jeff Widen and Jeff Singer, October 1993
Difficulty: III, 5.8, C1
Time: 6 hours
Equipment: 4 sets of Friends through #3; 3 #3.5 and #4 Friends;
2 sets of TCUs; 2 sets of stoppers; hooks

Approach: Chip Tower is an easy scramble from the White Rim Road. This route ascends the south face of the tower, following the obvious thin splitter in the middle of the face.

Route: Pitch 1: Begin atop loose blocks and climb 5.8 rock to a ledge on the left. Pitch 2: Continue up the splitter (C1) to a stance on the left. Pitch 3: A 5.8 chimney leads to the ridge. Pitch 4: Climb the bolt ladder/face to the summit.

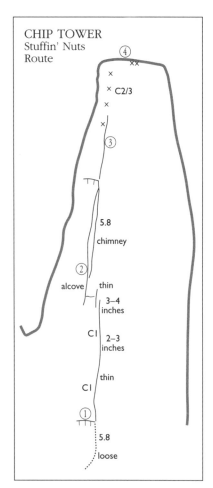

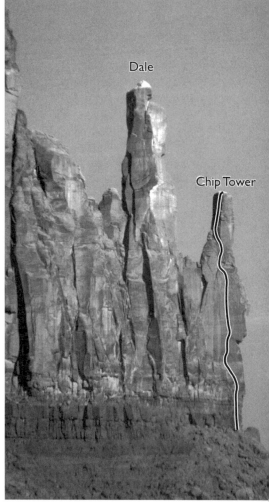

Climb 47, Chip Tower, Stuffin' Nuts.
© Cameron M. Burns.

Special considerations: The first ascent party used only a few pitons. Subsequent ascents will undoubtedly go clean, and free.

Descent: Make three double-rope rappels down the north face using fixed anchors already in place.

48 TIKI TOWER, BRAVE LITTLE TOASTER

First ascent: Jeff Widen and Mitch Allen (with Paul Frank and Fred Lifton working on pitch 1), November 1991

Difficulty: III, 5.9, C1

Time: 6 hours

Equipment: 3 sets of TCUs; 3 sets of camming units

Approach: From the parking spot on White Rim Road 15 miles from the Potash Road/Shafer Trail intersection, hike north up gullies and benches toward the tower. The walk takes roughly an hour. The route climbs a crack system starting on the right side of the southwest face that ends at a notch at the base of the main tower.

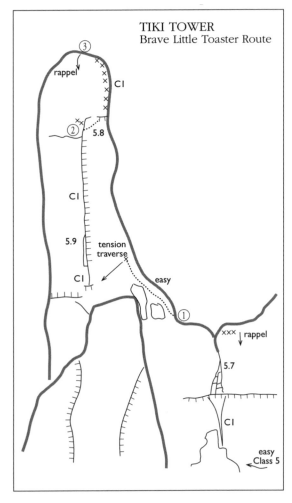

TIKI TOWER
Brave Little Toaster Route

Route: Pitch 1: Climb over blocks to a thin, right-leaning crack. Climb this (C1) to a ledge, then climb 5.7 cracks to the notch between Tiki Tower and the butte to the southeast. Pitch 2: Climb up easy blocks to the south corner of the tower, then tension-traverse left from a bolt to a stance at the base of a large, left-facing corner. Climb the corner (C1, with occasional free moves) to a sloping ledge with two bolts. Pitch 3: Face-climb right (5.8), around the tower to a stance on the east corner. Climb a six-bolt ladder to the summit.

Descent: Make one double-rope rappel to the notch at the top of pitch 1, then one to the ground.

Pitch 1, Brave Little Toaster, Tiki Tower, Canyonlands National Park. © Jeff Widen.

49 WASHER WOMAN, IN SEARCH OF SUDS

First ascent: Glenn Randall and Charlie Fowler, September 1982
Difficulty: III, 5.10+
Time: 6 hours
Equipment: 2 sets of Camalots; 1 set of TCUs; 1 set of wired stoppers;
15 quickdraws
     Approach: From the parking spot on the White Rim Road roughly 15.7 miles
from the Shafer Trail/Potash Road intersection, hike up past Monster Tower's south
face to the south face of Washer Woman. This route ascends the west face of the

Following pitch 4, In Search of Suds, Washer Woman, Canyonlands National Park. © Cameron M. Burns.

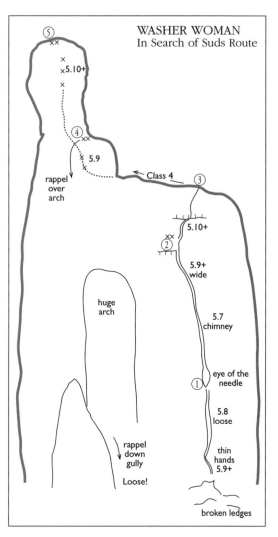

tower. Start by scrambling up into the notch between Monster Tower and Washer Woman, then move left (north) along ledges to a prominent crack/chimney system on the right (east) side of the west face.

Route: Pitch 1: Climb a stunning hand crack over a bulge (5.9+), then continue straight up a flaring chimney system (5.8) to a belay in a notch with an "eye" piercing the entire tower, where one can look down the east face. There are several slings looped through the "eye of the needle." Pitch 2: Climb into the eye and then move left into a hidden crack system that leads up and left, getting progressively harder. The pitch ends with a flaring slot, then perfect hand/fist jams up a bulge to reach a large, flat ledge and a two-bolt belay. Pitch 3: Climb straight up and slightly to the right over a bulge (5.10+), then straight up to the crest of the south ridge. Pitch 4: Climb a full rope length along the south ridge (mostly Class 4), then a

30-foot headwall (5.9) that leads to a belay below the final summit block. Pitch 5: Climb the summit block on the south side via a series of ledges that lead to a three-bolt face (5.10+) and the top of the tower.

Special considerations: The first pitch has some very loose blocks in it.

Descent: Make three double-rope rappels down the west face using the fixed anchors already in place. There are numerous sets of rappel anchors on the face, so the exact number of rappels and choice of anchors is up to the individual party. This is one of the wildest rappels in the desert, as it goes through Washer Woman's gigantic arch.

50 MONSTER TOWER, NORTH RIDGE

First ascents: Ken Trout and Kirk Miller, May 1981. *First free ascent:* Richard Harrison and Jay Smith, October 31, 1983.

Difficulty: III, 5.11a

Time: 1 full day

Equipment: 3 sets of camming units to #4; stoppers

Approach: From the White Rim Road, hike northwest around the base of Monster Tower's north face, past the Kor Route (climb 51), to the right side of the face. The hike takes about an hour. The route starts up a hand crack in a left-facing corner.

Route: Pitch 1: Climb the left-facing corner to the top of a flake and belay at fixed anchors (5.9). Pitch 2: Continue up a wandering crack to a ledge and belay (5.10+). Pitch 3: Climb the off-width ramp to the right, which ends at a decent ledge with fixed anchors (5.9). Pitch 4: Climb the obvious thin corner (5.11a), which widens to off-width, then belay at a ledge with fixed anchors. Pitch 5: Move left and climb a corner to the left of some broken rock; belay at another ledge with fixed anchors (5.9). Pitch 6: Move right, then climb a broken corner and then a roof to gain a ledge with fixed anchors (5.10). Pitch 7: Face-climb left of an old bolt ladder to the summit (5.11), or climb the bolt ladder, then scramble to the top.

Special considerations: Individual pitches can be broken up in various ways. Also, scrambling in from the notch between Monster Tower and Washer Woman

Chester Dreiman on the North Ridge, Monster Tower, Canyonlands.
© Ed Webster/Mountain Imagery.

is funky and kind of dangerous, especially in winter. If one goes this way, angle down and left to the north side of the ridge to join the third pitch's ramp. Pitches 6 and 7 of this climb are shown on the climb 51 map.

Descent: Rappel the route.

51 MONSTER TOWER, KOR ROUTE

First ascent: Layton Kor, Larry Dalke, and Cub Shafer, December 26, 1963. The variation to the first two pitches was climbed by Evelyn Lees and Rick Wyatt, spring 1986.

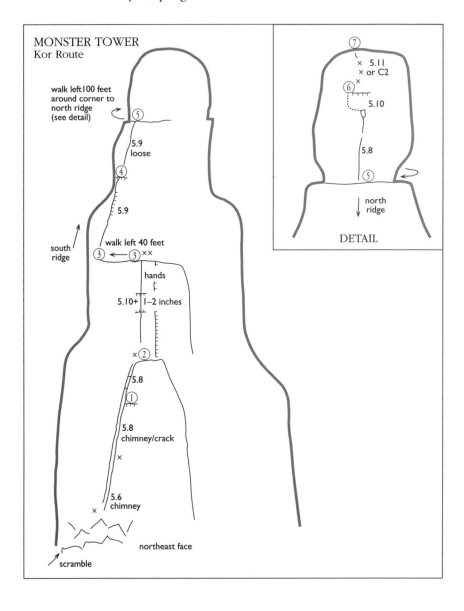

MONSTER TOWER
Kor Route

walk left 100 feet
around corner to
north ridge
(see detail)

⑤

5.9
loose

④

5.9

south
ridge

walk left 40 feet

③ ← ③ ××

hands

5.10+ 1–2 inches

×②

5.8

①

5.8
chimney/crack

×

5.6
chimney

×

northeast face

scramble

⑦

× 5.11
× or C2
×
⑥
5.10

⑤

5.8

⑤

north
ridge

DETAIL

Difficulty: IV, 5.10, C2
Time: 1 full day
Equipment: 2 sets of camming units to #4 with 3 #1.5 Friends; 1 set of TCUs; stoppers
Approach: From the White Rim Road, hike northwest to the base of Monster Tower's northeast face. The hike takes about an hour. The route begins on the northeast side of the tower, up a pile of loose blocks that lead to the base of a low-angled chimney, which forms the left side of a large, triangular-shaped pillar.

Route: Pitch 1: Climb the chimney (5.6) past a bolt, then continue (5.8) to a ledge with slings wrapped around a block. Pitch 2: Continue to the top of the pillar (5.8). Pitch 3: Climb a thin hand crack left of a left-facing corner (5.10+) to a dirt mantle and a big ledge with fixed anchors. Move the belay left 40 feet (Class 1) to the base of the south ridge. Pitch 4: Climb an obvious crack/corner (5.9) to a stance on a ledge. Pitch 5: Continue up the loose crack (5.9) to a large ledge. Walk left 100 feet to the left, around the tower to the north ridge. Pitch 6: Climb a crack past a fixed pin (5.8), then a thin crack (5.10) to its top. Move left on the face to a ledge. Pitch 7: Climb a bolt ladder, then face-climb to the top (C2).

Jeff Widen on pitch 3, Kor Route, Monster Tower. Photo: Rich McDonald/Widen collection.

Special considerations: This climb has tricky route-finding. None of the pitches' cracks are sustained at the same size. Even the crux pitch (pitch 3) is varied in size. Also, there is a good variation to pitch 1: start at the same place as the Kor Route, but climb to the left up a beautiful, thin hand crack (5.10) in a left-facing corner that ends near the top of the big shoulder (top of pitch 2).

Descent: Rappel the North Ridge (climb 50).

52 BLOCKTOP, ORIGINAL ROUTE

First ascent: Bryan Ferguson, Bill Ellwood, and Greg Doubek, October 11–12, 1985
Difficulty: IV, 5.10, C2
Time: 1 full day
Equipment: 2 sets of camming units through #5; 1 set of TCUs

Approach: From the road, the hike takes about an hour to Blocktop. Begin up a thin crack, which curves left and widens dramatically, below the left side of the north face.

Route: Pitch 1: Climb the crack through a pod to gain the ledge left of the tower, in the notch between it and Islet in the Sky (C2). Pitch 2: Move right 20 feet on a thin ledge (C1). Pitch 3: Climb a thin crack (C1) that widens to a hand crack (5.10), and belay at a ledge on the left. Pitch 4: Climb a hand crack as it widens to a fist crack/off-width, then worm into a chimney that brings one to a wild hanging belay at the lip of the final roof on the tower (5.10, C2). Pitch 5: A 5.6 chimney leads to the summit.

Special considerations: This route will likely go entirely free, if it hasn't already.

Descent: Rappel the route.

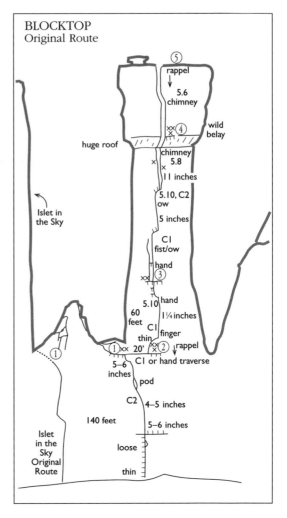

BLOCKTOP
Original Route

53 ISLET IN THE SKY, ORIGINAL ROUTE

First ascents: Ken Trout and Bruce Lella, 1976. *First clean ascent:* Steve Bartlett, 1996.

Difficulty: IV, 5.10, C3+

Time: 1 full day

Equipment: 3 sets of camming units to #3 Camalot; 2 sets of TCUs; 3 sets of RPs with extra #1, #2, and #3; 3 sets of stoppers; a selection of hooks

Approach: From the road, the hike takes about an hour to Islet in the Sky.

Route: Pitch 1: Climb a wandering hand and fist crack on the rock wall separating Islet in the Sky from Blocktop, to the notch between the two towers (5.10). Pitch 2: Move up and left to the base of the main tower. Pitch 3: Work left along a horizontal seam (C1). Pitches 4–5: Climb a thin seam up the north face to a sling

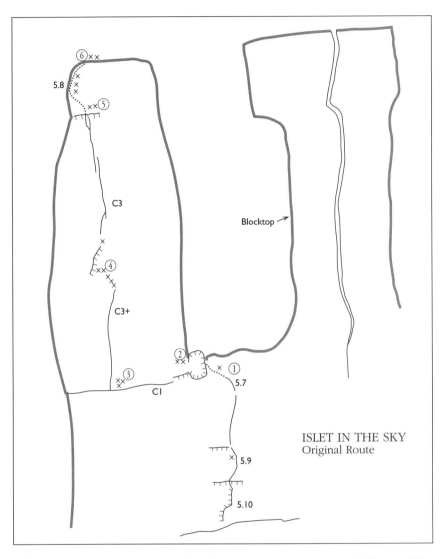

belay; continue to a stance on the shoulder, using many stoppers and RP nuts (C3+, C3). Pitch 6: A bolt ladder leads to the summit (5.8).

Special considerations: Bolts atop pitch 4 need replacing.

Descent: Rappel the route.

54 STANDING ROCK, KOR ROUTE

First ascents: Layton Kor, Steve Komito, and Huntley Ingalls, October 13–15, 1962. *First solo ascent:* John Middendorf, June 1991. *First free ascent:* Keith Reynolds and Walt Shipley, October 26, 1993.

Difficulty: III, 5.10, C1 or III, 5.11c

Time: 5 hours

Equipment: 2 sets of Camalots to #4; 1 set of TCUs; 3 sets of wired stoppers; 20 quickdraws

Approach: The recommended approach is on the north side of Monument Basin (the side you first get to in driving there on the White Rim Road), where there is a

Climb 54, Standing Rock, Kor Route.
© Cameron M. Burns.

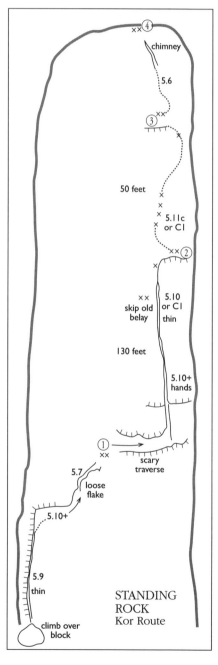

thin peninsula of land that juts out on the eastern side of the basin. On the south-west side of this peninsula, an old shepherd's trail (it may require some hunting around to find) leads down into the basin. From the south side of the basin, where a similar peninsula of land juts north into the basin, on the east side of this peninsula (near a car turnaround area), one can also scramble down. This route starts on the north side of the tower.

Route: Pitch 1: Climb the dihedral (5.9) to the roof, then traverse to the right for 20 feet and turn the corner. Continue up and right for 50 feet to a comfortable belay ledge with numerous fixed anchors. Pitch 2: Traverse right, on the large ledge at the belay level, for 25 feet (5.7) to an obvious vertical crack. Climb straight up the crack for 130 feet (5.10+), bypassing an old hanging belay on your left. The pitch ends on a spacious ledge, just below the crux of the route. Pitch 3: Climb the crux (5.11c or C1). There are several good stopper placements before a long, awkward reach up to an old bolt. Climb past the old bolt ladder to another spacious ledge (50 feet above the last belay), which leads off to the right. Pitch 4: Follow the ledge right, then scramble up to the summit (5.6).

Special considerations: On the first pitch, the leader should protect the second climber by leaving several pieces of gear under the roof traverse but, at the same time, use long runners to cut down on rope drag.

Descent: Make four double-rope rappels down the west face using fixed anchors. There are numerous sets of rappel anchors on the face, so the exact number of rappels and choice of anchors is up to the individual party.

55 SHARK'S FIN, FETISH ARÊTE

First ascents: Rob Slater, Jim Bodenhamer, Bruce Hunter, and Tom Cotter, May 1992. *First free ascent:* Stevie Haston, Steve Bartlett, and Laurence Gouault (5.10+), April 6, 1996.
Difficulty: III, 5.10+ R
Time: 6 hours
Equipment: 2 sets of Camalots; 2 sets of TCUs; 1 set of wired stoppers
Approach: The recommended approach is on the north side of Monument Basin (the side you first get to in driving there on the White Rim Road), where there is a thin peninsula of land that juts out on the eastern side of the basin. On the south-west side of this peninsula, an old shepherd's trail (it may require some hunting around to find) leads down into the basin. From the south side of the basin, where a similar peninsula of land juts north into the basin, on the east side of this peninsula (near a car turnaround area), one can also scramble down. The Shark's Fin is the striking tower just south of a large butte (Bruce Smith Tower) that sits south of Standing Rock. This route ascends the southern, low-angled prow of the Shark's Fin, beginning on the left side of the prow, at the junction of the south and west faces of the tower.

Route: Pitch 1: Climb past a wide (4-inch-plus) crack just right of the south-west arête up to a small stance on the arête (5.10a). Pitch 2: Traverse left around the corner, zigzag up and left up a crack system that peters out into large, steep, loose blocks. Before these blocks are reached, leave the crack and traverse 20 feet

left to an easy dihedral system, which soon gains the large ledge/shoulder (5.10b R). Pitch 3: Climb up the arête, over a bulge at 50 feet, then move to the right to avoid a bigger, looser bulge. Belay on a ledge just below a second ledge (5.10c). Pitch 4: Walk along the ledge, then up past a couple of fixed anchors (crux), then easier climbing up and left over steep, juggy terrain to a short, bulging crack that gains a good ledge on the main shoulder. Belay on the curiously balanced block above (5.10d). Pitch 5: Climb easy terrain to the summit, except for one irritating mantel (5.7).

Special considerations: This route has some dangerous and run-out climbing. Originally rated A2 and climbed with just two pitons, this route has reportedly also been done clean at 5.10-, C2.

Descent: Rappel the route.

Shark's Fin, Monument Basin, Canyonlands National Park. Fetish Arête climbs the left, low-angled side of the tower as seen in this view. © Cameron M. Burns.

SHAFER CANYON

56 BIRD'S VIEW BUTTE, UNEMPLOYMENT LINE
First ascent: Mike Pennings and Drew Spaulding, October 1993
Difficulty: III, 5.11-
Time: 1 full day
Equipment: 2 sets of camming units to #4 Camalots; 1 set of TCUs; 1 set of stoppers
Approach: From the parking spot near the canyon edge directly north of the Crow's Head Spires, on a promontory of land jutting toward the spires (4.1 miles from Island in the Sky Road), walk south to the point of land directly north of the spires and scramble down broken ledges and boulders to locate the rap anchors leading to the canyon floor below. These ledges are very exposed and the anchors require a little bit of searching to find; a belay might be a good idea. Three ropes are needed for fixing if one descends here. If you cannot find the anchors, bring enough gear so you can set your own anchors down the cliff. If you cannot find the rap anchors at

the tip of the promontory, look west from the point and locate a large tree 150 feet west of the point. Another descent begins here (bring three ropes to fix). From the bottom of the rappels, to reach Unemployment Line, head south, past Crow's Head Spires (the first twin-summitted butte south of the promontory) to the next large butte, Bird's View Butte. Unemployment Line climbs the northeast face, starting 300 feet left of the northernmost point of the butte.

Route: Pitch 1: Starting 30 feet left of a large triangular flake, climb a V-slot to

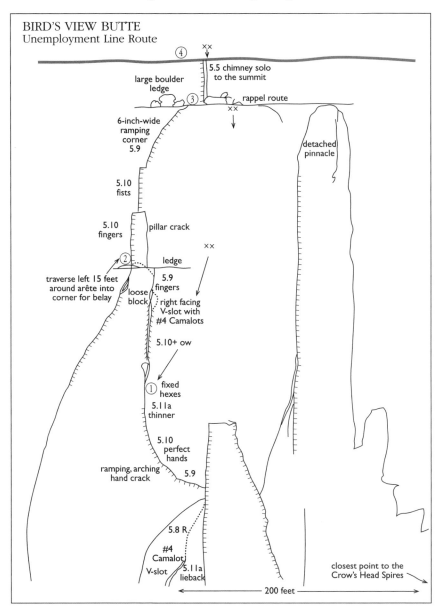

BIRD'S VIEW BUTTE
Unemployment Line Route

Climb 56, Bird's View Butte, Unemployment Line. © Cameron M. Burns.

a 5.11a layback, then run-out 5.8 rock to the left side of the flake. Follow a ramping, perfect hand crack (5.10) as it thins (5.11a) and gains the base of an off-width. Belay at fixed hexcentric nuts. Pitch 2: Climb the off-width above the belay (5.10+) past some loose blocks, then a 5.9 finger crack to a ledge. Move left 15 feet around an arête to a belay. Pitch 3: Climb a finger crack to a fist crack (5.10), then gain a ramping corner (5.9) system that leads to a large ledge. Pitch 4: Climb a 5.5 chimney to the summit.

Special considerations: This route was the first ascent of the tower.

Descent: Rappel fixed anchors to the right of the route. The first ascent party suggests carrying a bolt kit to replace poor anchors.

TUSHER AND MILL CANYONS AND COURTHOUSE PASTURE

Tusher and Mill Canyons are two parallel, north-south canyons that lie northwest of Moab, on the west side of US 191 and north of Hwy. 313. The short, narrow canyons culminate at their southeastern ends in a wide-open, very enchanting area called Courthouse Pasture, which is as beautiful as any area in the desert. The area offers excellent midwinter climbing and camping because the narrow canyons provide much shelter from cold winter winds.

The rock here is Entrada sandstone, the same kind found in Arches National Park, sitting atop a layer of crumbling brown Dewey Bridge formation sandstone (a type of Entrada). While the Dewey Bridge layer can be loose and awful, it's the Entrada above that offers excellent climbing on some stunning formations.

Area climbing regulations: The routes in Tusher and Mill Canyons and the Courthouse Pasture lie on public land, managed by the Bureau of Land Management (BLM). There are no restrictions on climbing at present, although it is up to all climbers to leave as little impact as possible so that this policy remains.

Special considerations: This area has been hammered by four-wheel-drive enthusiasts driving all over the place, hence there are numerous roads plowing across the delicate sand and flora. Please stick to existing roads to reach the towers. There are enough roads to get you to these climbs without making new ones.

Getting there: From Moab drive north on US 191 4.5 miles past the intersection with Hwy. 313 (the road to Dead Horse Point and Canyonlands National Park) to a small dirt road, the Mill Canyon Road, and turn left onto Mill Canyon Road. This road is hard to spot on your first visit. From the north on I-70, take exit 180 and drive south on US 191 exactly 16.3 miles to Mill Canyon Road, and turn right.

Cross the railroad tracks and follow Mill Canyon Road west for about 0.6 mile. At this point, the Mill Canyon Road veers left, while the road to Tusher Canyon veers right. At the split, take the left fork for 0.5 mile, then veer right, following the signs to Mill Canyon. Drive another 1.6 miles through the canyon. The road can be extremely rough, but most four-wheel-drive vehicles can make the trip easily. After 1.6 miles from the second split, a dirt road veers off right; go straight, and continue south for another 1.2 miles. (As you progress along this road, it seems as though you will bypass Echo Pinnacle altogether.) At 1.2 miles, turn right, onto a smaller dirt road, and follow this west, past the northern side of Echo Pinnacle. When you are almost directly north of the tower (after about 0.4 mile from the last turn), several small roads lead south (left) and very close to the base of the tower. Follow whichever one your vehicle can make. They all end up on a white rock bench below the tower. It is only a short walk to the base of the tower.

To reach The House of Putterman from Echo Pinnacle, continue west on the dirt road that lies north of Echo Pinnacle, through a natural gate in the mesa to the west, for about 1.4 miles, then turn left. The House of Putterman is the obvious butte to the southeast. Drive as close to the butte as possible, and park. It is only a short walk to the base of the tower.

It is also possible to reach Echo Pinnacle and The House of Putterman via Tusher Canyon, the next north-south canyon west of Mill Canyon. From US 191, drive 0.6 mile west on Mill Canyon Road, but at the fork, instead of veering left toward Mill Canyon, veer right and follow the road another 2.1 miles to an intersection. Turn left into Tusher Canyon. Tusher Canyon offers a better way (less rough) to reach the Courthouse Pasture area, but the road is extremely narrow, and anything wider than a Toyota four-wheel-drive truck might have problems. Drive 1.9 miles down Tusher Canyon. A road veers off left. This road leads to Echo Pinnacle and the Courthouse Pasture area. To reach Echo Pinnacle, follow it for 1.4 miles. To reach The House of Putterman, go straight and the butte is obvious on a hill to the left.

Charlie French following pitch 3, Window Route, Echo Pinnacle, Mill Canyon.
© Cameron M. Burns.

To reach Monitor and Merrimac Buttes from Echo Pinnacle (the best way to access the two buttes), drive south on Mill Canyon Road another 1.1 miles, to a five-way intersection. Merrimac Butte is directly ahead of you. Take the road leading slightly left and ahead (not the sharp left that is possible) and veer around the northeastern side of Merrimac Butte on a rock shelf. The east face comes quickly into view and is just a short hike from the car. The southwestern corner of Monitor Butte is just a short drive to the south, on the same rock shelf. Likewise, it is a short hike from the car.

57 ECHO PINNACLE, WINDOW ROUTE

First ascent: Eric Bjørnstad, Ken Wyrick, and Terry McKenna, 1974
Difficulty: II–III, 5.10d/11a or II–III, 5.8, C1
Time: ½ day
Equipment: 2 sets of camming units with extra #2 to #3; 20 quickdraws

Approach: From whichever dirt road you take toward the tower, it is only a short walk to the base of the tower. This route ascends the left side of the west face of Echo Pinnacle, passing the huge "window" that pierces the tower about 100 feet above the ground.

Route: Pitch 1: Climb loose, dirty rock (5.8) via thin cracks straight to the window, bypassing an old bolt on the way. Belay in the window. Pitch 2: Climb straight up for 80 feet via the obvious 3-inch crack above the window (5.10+/5.11- or C1) passing two old bolts to a sling belay. Pitch 3: Climb the bolt ladder above to the summit.

West faces of Echo Pinnacle: climb 57, Window Route, and climb 58, No Reply.
© Cameron M. Burns.

Special Considerations: The original route climbed the east face to the window. The Window Route (not recommended) is 5.9 and protection is difficult.

Descent: Make two double-rope rappels down the center of the west face using the fixed anchors already in place.

58 ECHO PINNACLE, NO REPLY

First ascent: Mike Baker and Leslie Henderson, April 1992
Difficulty: III, 5.9, A2
Time: 1 day
Equipment: 2 sets of camming units with 1 extra #0.5; 1 set of technical Friends; a selection of 12 pitons, from Lost Arrows to ¾-inch angles
Approach: From whichever dirt road you take toward the tower, it is only a short walk to the base of the tower. This route follows the prominent crack system at the south end of the west face.

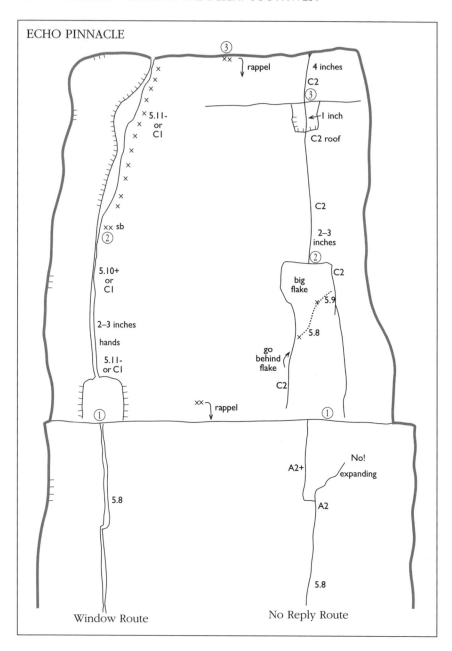

Route: Pitch 1: Climb loose 5.8/A2+ (Dewey Bridge) rock directly below a large flake to the ledge separating the Dewey Bridge sandstone from the Entrada rock above. Pitch 2: Move left, then climb C2 rock until it's possible to move up behind the flake. Behind the flake, climb 5.9 rock past two bolts, and move right, to the right (south) side of the flake. Mantle (C2) up onto the top of the flake. Pitch 3:

Clean aid the crack above the flake (C2) over a roof, then belay in a flare. Pitch 4: Climb the 4-inch crack above the flare to the summit (C2).

Special considerations: Above the first pitch, all the aid is clean aid. This route will likely go free in the future. Also, to avoid the "non-clean" nailing, it's possible to climb the first pitch of the Window Route (climb 57), then traverse right 80 feet to the base of No Reply's second pitch and climb the route from there.

Descent: Make two double-rope rappels down the center of the west face using the fixed anchors already in place.

59 THE HOUSE OF PUTTERMAN, WALDEN'S ROOM

First ascents: Cameron Burns and Brian Takei, October 22, 1994.
First free ascent: Jon Butler and Cameron Burns, October 22, 1995.
Difficulty: II–III, 5.10+
Time: 3 hours
Equipment: 1 set of camming units, 1 set of TCUs
Approach: From where you parked, it is only a short walk to the base of the tower. The Walden's Room route lies on the east face, the face opposite the road. The route

Climb 59, The House of Putterman, Walden's Room. © Cameron M. Burns.

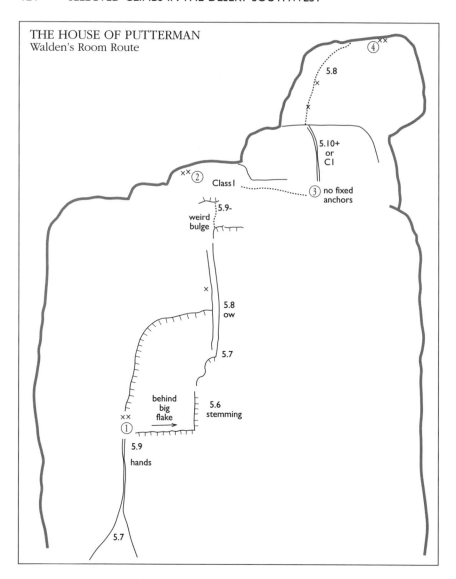

THE HOUSE OF PUTTERMAN
Walden's Room Route

4

5.8

5.10+
or
C1

② Class I .... ③ no fixed
anchors

5.9-
weird
bulge

5.8
ow

5.7

behind
big
flake

5.6
stemming

①

5.9
hands

5.7

begins up a soft, low-angling block that sits in a prominent corner near the south end of the east face.

Route: Pitch 1: Climb up the left side of the block (5.7) to a hand crack in a corner (5.9). Pitch 2: Walk right (north) 20 feet to the obvious chimney, and climb it (5.8) to the top, then go straight up over a bulge (5.9-) to a fixed belay. Pitch 3: Scramble north 100 feet on weird, flat platforms to the east side of the final tower. (There are no fixed anchors at this belay.) Pitch 4: Climb a short finger crack (5.10+), then continue up a bolted face (5.8) to the summit.

Descent: Make one short rappel off the summit tower, then scramble back down to the top of pitch 2. Make one double-rope rappel to the ground.

60 MONITOR BUTTE, THE PLUNGE

First ascents: Ron Olevsky and Dave Mondeau, May 1986. *First free ascent:* Earl Wiggins, Katy Cassidy, and Peter Gallagher, February 1988.

Difficulty: II, 5.12a

Time: 4 hours

Equipment: 3 sets of camming units with extra #1.5 and #2; 2 sets of TCUs

Approach: Veer around the northeastern side of Merrimac Butte on a rock shelf. From where you parked, the east face is just a short hike; continue to the southwest corner of the butte. The route ascends the striking crack and right-facing corner system just east (right) of the southwestern corner of the butte.

Route: Pitch 1: Climb along the obvious ledge that leads into the crack system, then climb with fingers and hands up the slowly widening crack (5.12a or C1). Pitch 2: Climb the off-width above (5.11 or C1) to the top of the butte. Pitch 3: Scramble east on the summit platform to the highest point. A boulder move gets one on top.

Descent: Make two double-rope rappels down the route.

Monitor Butte's west face. The Plunge follows the obvious crack system in the pillar on the left. © Cameron M. Burns.

61 MERRIMAC BUTTE, WITHOUT A NET

First ascent: Charlie Fowler and Sue Wint, April 1991

Difficulty: II, 5.8

Time: 4 hours

Equipment: 1 set of camming units; 1 set of stoppers

Approach: From where you parked, the southwest corner of Monitor Butte is a short hike; continue around to the east face of the Merrimac. The route ascends the wide chimney system behind the Paddle Wheel, a large buttress on the east face just a few hundred feet from the north (right) end of the butte.

Route: Pitch 1: Start up the off-width (5.6) and belay at a stance with fixed anchors. Pitches 2–3: Continue up the chimney and left (5.8), belaying at fixed

East faces of Merrimac Butte: climb 61, Without a Net; climb 62, Hypercrack on the Anchor Chain. © Cameron M. Burns.

anchors. Pitch 4: Move up and right to gain the summit plateau (Class 4).

Descent: Walk to the right, approximately 100 feet, to the top of a route called Merrymaker (lying between Without a Net and Hypercrack on the Anchor Chain, climb 62). Make two double-rope rappels down Merrymaker.

62 MERRIMAC BUTTE, HYPERCRACK ON THE ANCHOR CHAIN

First ascent: Jimmy Dunn, John Bouchard, Eric Bjørnstad, and Lin Ottinger, September 22, 1985. (Jeff Widen led the first pitch prior to the complete ascent.)

Difficulty: II, 5.11

Time: 2 hours

Equipment: 1 set of regular camming units; a selection of extra-large camming devices

Approach: From where you parked, the southwest corner of Monitor Butte is a short hike; continue around to the east face of the Merrimac. The route ascends the striking crack on the northeast corner of the butte, 200 feet to the right of Without a Net (climb 61).

Route: Pitch 1: Start up the low-angling crack, then fist-jam over the roof to fixed anchors (5.11). Pitch 2: Continue up the ever-widening crack (5.11) until it becomes possible to squeeze inside. The pitch ends at the top of the butte.

Descent: Walk left, approximately 100 feet, to the top of a route called Merrymaker. Make two double-rope rappels down Merrymaker.

WALL STREET/POTASH ROAD

Wall Street (also known as Potash Road) has become one of Moab's premier cragging areas, ever since route development began there in the mid-1980s. Like Indian Creek Canyon and certain areas of the San Rafael Swell, Wall Steet offers hundreds of routes.

King's Hand is one of the more prominent and unique features along Wall Street, and the climbing on it is representative of the Wall Street area: sandy, slabby, sometimes run out, and an interesting jaunt above thundering trucks headed to and from the potash mine at the end of the road.

Area climbing regulations: The routes along Potash Road lie on public land, managed by the Bureau of Land Management (BLM). There are no restrictions on climbing at present, although it is up to all climbers to leave as little impact as possible so that this policy remains.

Getting there: The Potash Road (a.k.a. Wall Street) follows the Colorado River west from Moab. From Moab, drive north on US 191 past Hwy. 128 (River Road) 1.7 miles, and turn left onto Hwy. 279. From the north on I-70, take exit 180 and drive south on US 191 to Hwy. 279, then turn right onto Hwy. 279 (Potash Road). Drive exactly 4.4 miles on Hwy. 279 to a small parking area on the right. The King's Hand is obvious lying against the canyon wall north of the parking lot's outhouse.

63 KING'S HAND, KING'S HAND LEFT

First ascent: Bego Gerhardt and Barry Miller, September 8, 1987
Difficulty: III, 5.9
Time: ½ day
Equipment: Small Friends; TCUs; stoppers
Approach: From the parking lot, walk down the canyon (west) a short distance until

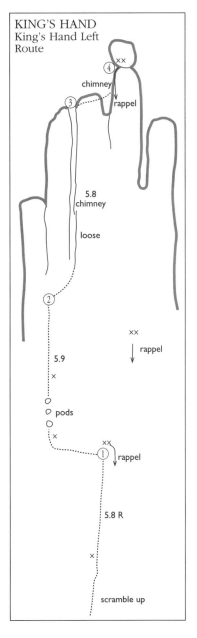

KING'S HAND
King's Hand Left
Route

4 xx
chimney
3 rappel

5.8
chimney

loose

2

xx
rappel

5.9
x

pods

xx
rappel

5.8 R

x

scramble up

Climb 63, King's Hand, King's Hand Left. © Cameron M. Burns.

it is possible to scramble up to the base of the King's Hand.

    Route: Pitch 1: Begin up a trough just right of center on the back of the hand (the side facing the road) past a bolt to a belay (5.8 R). Pitch 2: Move left 30 feet just under a red band in the rock, then climb past several pods into another trough, which leads to a belay (5.9). Pitch 3: Climb up and slightly right, and work into a loose chimney between two of the fingers (the second finger down from the deformed "summit finger" and the third finger down from the deformed "summit finger"). Continue to a belay at the top of the third finger (5.8). Pitch 3: Work up behind the top fingers to rappel anchors below the summit block (5.8). The summit block can be climbed by throwing a rope over it and belaying the climber using a top rope.

Descent: Make three double-rope rappels down the front of the hand.

KANE CREEK

Kane Creek is a long, interesting canyon that takes off south from the Colorado River just southwest of Moab, stretching more than 20 miles south before turning east into the hills and mesas around Hole in the Rock, located south of Moab on US 191.

Kane Creek is perhaps most fascinating for its remarkable variety of rock types and rock climbs. From "mini" big walls to short splitters to weird Cutler sandstone towers reminiscent of the Fisher Towers, Kane Creek seems to have everyone's version of "desert rock."

In this guidebook, only a few routes—all of impeccable quality—are described. Two of these routes, Playing Hooky and Stairway to Heaven, are in an area called The Tombstones (a.k.a. The Cirque of the Climbables), an area of "mini" big walls in Wingate sandstone. In contrast, The Predator and Shelbyville are formations at the "bottom end" of the canyon, in Cutler sandstone.

Area climbing regulations: The routes in the Kane Creek valley lie on public land, managed by the Bureau of Land Management (BLM). There are no restrictions on climbing at present, although it is up to all climbers to leave as little impact as possible so that this policy remains.

Getting there: From downtown Moab, drive along Main Street (US 191) to the McDonald's and turn west onto Kane Creek Road. Follow the road through the Moab suburbs, then along the south side of the Colorado River for 4.8 miles until the road crosses a cattle guard and turns into a dirt road. At this point, it dips down into Kane Creek Canyon proper. From the cattle guard, drive 0.5 mile down Kane Creek Canyon, and The Tombstones are obvious on the left. There are three of them: Left, Center, and Right. Park along the roadside.

To reach The Predator, continue past The Tombstones down Kane Creek Road for roughly 4.5 miles from the cattle guard (roughly 4 miles past The Tombstones), to the point where the valley opens up wide to the south. Park along the roadside. The Predator is located across the valley to the southwest, and can be very difficult to locate from the road because it blends into the cliffs behind it. It sits at the end of a large, pronounced point of Cutler sandstone many hundreds of feet high.

Shelbyville is much easier to reach. Continue on Kane Creek Road for 6.5 miles from the cattle guard; Shelbyville, a prominent Cutler sandstone butte that looks like a wide wall from the road, is on your right. There are several dirt tracks that lead off to the right (west) and access the back of Shelbyville. If you follow the correct track, it's possible to drive to within 100 feet of Mr. Putterman Goes to Washington. Finding the correct track requires a few minutes of trying different tracks.

64 CENTER TOMBSTONE, PLAYING HOOKY

First ascent: Jimmy Dunn, Charlie Fowler, Peter Verchick, Kevin Chase, and Betsy McKittrick, May 1993

Difficulty: IV, 5.10, C2 or IV, 5.12

Time: 1–2 days

Equipment: 2 sets of Friends; 2 sets of TCUs; 2 sets of stoppers; 2 sets of Lowe Balls

Approach: From the road, hike 10 minutes to The Tombstones. Playing Hooky climbs the obvious crack system in the center of the Center Tombstone.

Route: Pitch 1: Climb a 5.7 chimney that leads up and right, to fixed anchors. Pitch 2: Move up and right, to an obvious hand crack, and climb it to a sling belay (5.10+). Pitch 3: Continue up the crack system to a sling belay under a small roof (5.12 or C1). Pitch 4: Continue up the crack system to a sling belay to the left of a triangular roof (5.12- or C1). Pitch 5: Continue up a right-facing corner to a sling belay (C2). Pitch 6: Aid out the bulge to the summit of the Center Tombstone (C2).

Special considerations: This route has been climbed completely clean by Dave

The Tombstones on Kane Creek: climb 64, Center Tombstone, Playing Hooky; climb 65, Right Tombstone, Stairway to Heaven. © Cameron M. Burns.

Medara and Mike Pennings (October 1994). The 5.12 climbing is not mandatory. The route will likely go entirely free.

Descent: Rappel the route, leaving ropes fixed on the last three pitches so you can pull into rap anchors.

65   RIGHT TOMBSTONE, STAIRWAY TO HEAVEN

First ascent: Jimmy Dunn, Bob Novellino, Betsy McKittrick, Peter Verchick, Bret Sutteer, and Jay Smith, September 1994
Difficulty: III, 5.10+
Time: 1 full day
Equipment: 2 sets of camming units; 2 sets of TCUs; stoppers; wide gear (8"–10") for pitch 4
Approach: From the road, hike 10 minutes to The Tombstones. In the middle right center of the Right Tombstone is a faint arête. Stairway to Heaven climbs this arête to gain the obvious chimney just right of center on the wall above.

Route: Pitch 1: Climb the varying crack system of the crest of the arête as it passes through several layers of rock and a roof, then gains a ledge with fixed anchors (5.9+). Pitch 2: Climb a thin crack in the obvious left-facing, slightly low-angled corner, then move up and right, out of the corner, to climb the face to the right (5.10) on the crest of the arête. Pitch 3: Climb broken edges and corners to the top of a pillar leaning against the wall (5.8). Pitch 4: Move right, onto the obvious chimney, and climb a long pitch to a fixed belay in the chimney (5.10+). Pitch 5: Move left into a thin crack and climb it for 50 feet to a fixed anchor at the top.

Special considerations: Jimmy Dunn has a hard time naming routes and changes route names frequently. This route has also been called Jimmy's Chimney and For Desert Rats Only.

Descent: Rappel the route.

66   THE PREDATOR, REIGN OF TERROR

First ascent: Kyle Copeland and Eric Johnson, August 17, 1990
Difficulty: I, 5.11a
Time: 3 hours
Equipment: 1 set of camming units, with extra #1 and #2; 1 set of wired stoppers; 10 quickdraws
Approach: From the road, hike west 15 minutes across the valley to The Predator. The Predator

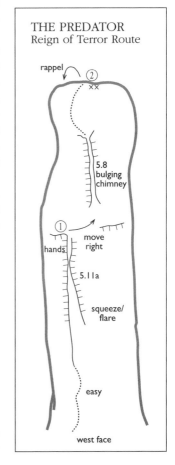

THE PREDATOR
Reign of Terror Route

rappel

②
xx

5.8
bulging
chimney

①   move
right
hands

5.11a

squeeze/
flare

easy

west face

is obvious; it stands at the leading edge of some large Cutler sandstone walls. Early afternoon is the best time to see it. In the morning it can blend in rather well. Start at the bottom of the west side of the tower.

Route: Pitch 1: Climb up the obvious flaring crack system (5.11a) to a ledge. Pitch 2: Move right and squeeze up a chimney (5.8) to the summit.

Descent: Make one double-rope rappel down the north face.

Climb 66, The Predator, Reign of Terror. © Cameron M. Burns.

67 SHELBYVILLE, MR. PUTTERMAN GOES TO WASHINGTON

First ascent: Cameron Burns and Jesse "The Body" Harvey, February 21, 1998
Difficulty: I, 5.9+, A1
Time: 3 hours
Equipment: 2 sets of camming units, with extra #4 and #5; 1 set of wired stoppers
Approach: From where you parked, within 100 feet of the route, start at the bottom of the southwest side of the tower. Look for rappel slings on the ridge to the right (south) of the summit. The route starts in the long crack system that descends from the ridge to the ground, just right of the slings, and climbs this low-angled crack system on the southwest side of the butte.
Route: Pitch 1: Climb up a ramp/corner system (5.9+, C1, will go free) to the ridge and fixed anchors. Pitch 2: Climb a short wall past two old bolts, then move to

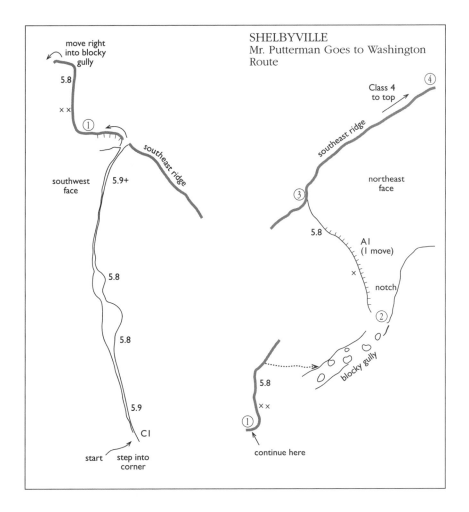

SHELBYVILLE
Mr. Putterman Goes to Washington
Route

move right into blocky gully

5.8

x x

①

southwest face

5.9+

southeast ridge

5.8

5.8

5.9

C1

start   step into corner

Class 4 to top

④

southeast ridge

③

northeast face

5.8

A1 (1 move)

x

notch

②

blocky gully

5.8

x x

①

continue here

Climb 67, Shelbyville, Mr. Putterman Goes to Washington. © Cameron M. Burns.

the right and scramble up a block-filled chimney on the right (northeast) side of the butte to belay at a notch. Pitch 3: Move up and left past a bolt to easier ground. Pitch 4: Walk to the summit.

Special considerations: This route will go clean and free in the near future.

Descent: From the summit, walk south, then rappel the route.

SOUTHEASTERN UTAH

BIG INDIAN WASH

Big Indian Rock, which lies near the Lisbon Valley Industrial Area between Moab and Indian Creek, is just one of hundreds of spires and buttes that are off the main roads surrounding Moab. Big Indian Rock is perhaps more noticeable than many of these other formations because it appears so striking from US 191. In reality, Big Indian Rock is a fin of rock, not a tower, but it is worth a visit if you have time, or are looking to do a route that doesn't see too much traffic.

Area climbing regulations: Big Indian Rock lies on public land, managed by the Bureau of Land Management (BLM). There are no restrictions on climbing at present, although it is up to all climbers to leave as little impact as possible so that this policy remains.

Getting there: Drive south from Moab on US 191 toward its intersection with Hwy. 46 (La Sal Junction). Continue south on US 191 another 13.1 miles to San Juan County Rd. 106 on the left (east), leading to the Lisbon Valley Industrial Area. (There are two roads leading to the Lisbon Valley Industrial Area; this is the second, or southernmost, of the two.) Follow San Juan County Rd. 106 east for exactly 8.2 miles. Big Indian Rock is obvious on the right (south) side of the road.

68 BIG INDIAN ROCK, ORIGINAL ROUTE
First ascents: Ken Wyrick and Carol Harden, April 1973. *First free ascent:* Bret Ruckman and Tim Coats (who did a variation to the original line), 1990.

Climb 68, Big Indian Rock, Original Route. © Cameron M. Burns.

Difficulty: II, 5.11, or 5.9, C1
Time: ½ day
Equipment: 1 set of Friends; 2 sets of TCUs; tie-offs for bolt studs
Approach: From the road, hike 10 minutes to the base of the rock, then around to its south face. The Original Route lies on the far left side of the south face, and follows a thin crack (adorned with bolts) just to the right of the west (left) end of the tower.
Route: Pitch 1: Climb the obvious thin crack to a ledge bypassing many bolts (5.11 or 5.8, C1). Pitch 2: Move right, then climb a low-angled corner with bolts on the face to the right (5.9, C1). Pitch 3: Scramble over to the summit.
Descent: Rappel the route.

INDIAN CREEK CANYON

No book on desert climbing would be complete without Supercrack, the route on Supercrack Buttress that changed desert climbing forever. In the fall of 1976, three cars loaded with Colorado Springs climbers headed west, into the desert. In one automobile were Jimmy Dunn (who had first spotted an "absolutely straight-up, parallel-sided crack" while climbing North Six Shooter in the winter of 1974–75 with Doug Snively) and two youngsters, Ed Webster and Bryan Becker. In a second car were Earl Wiggins and his late wife, Cheryl. And in a third car were Michael Gardner, Stewart Green, and Dennis Jackson, who had come along ostensibly to make a film of the ascent.

The climbers arrived in the canyon and waited until early afternoon, when the light on the chocolate-colored wall had softened, before beginning their ascent. By this time, Dunn had decided there were too many people around, and headed off to look at petroglyphs with Cheryl. Armed with a rack of hexcentrics and a couple of primitive, single-prong Lowe camming devices, Wiggins led the first pitch; Webster led the second; and then Becker followed both pitches together on a 9-millimeter haul rope. Then Wiggins led the third pitch all the way to the canyon's rim. "It wasn't complete unless we got to the rim," noted Webster recently.

Ironically, while Supercrack was climbed all the way to the canyon rim, it started a trend in which cracks were climbed for their quality and, especially in Indian Creek Canyon, often only to a rappel station a rope length up the wall. Today, most climbers who do Supercrack only climb the first pitch of the original route.

In the years following Supercrack, hundreds of routes have been climbed in Indian Creek Canyon, and only a small percentage of them actually reach the canyon rim. The Indian Creek Canyon style has now been adopted in every major desert climbing area, from Zion National Park to Colorado National Monument.

While there are literally thousands of routes in Indian Creek Canyon, scattered along hundreds of miles of canyon walls, there are far too many to squash into one single guidebook, let alone an overview book like this. Hence, a sampling of the best routes on Supercrack Buttress and a handful of routes on various Indian Creek Canyon towers are included here.

Area climbing regulations: The routes in Indian Creek Canyon lie on a mixture of public and private land. There are no restrictions on climbing at present, although it is up to all climbers to leave as little impact as possible so that this policy remains.

Special considerations: The routes on Supercrack Buttress are some of the most popular routes in the desert. Share them politely.

Getting there: Indian Creek Canyon is located about 40 miles south of Moab. To reach it, drive south on US 191 from Moab for roughly 42 miles. Then turn right, onto Hwy. 211, and reset your odometer.

Follow Hwy. 211 for 13.4 miles and pass Newspaper Rock (a small wall with numerous Anasazi petroglyphs) on the right. Continue 4.2 miles past Newspaper Rock (17.6 miles from US 191), and the Supercrack Buttress is on the right buttress, above the road.

To reach the Bridger Jack spires (Thumbelina and Sunflower Tower), drive another 4.3 miles past Supercrack Buttress (21.9 miles from US 191) and turn left onto the Beef Basin Road. Follow the Beef Basin Road for 0.9 mile, cross a cattle guard, then make a sharp right onto a rough road (although two-wheel drives can make it along this road most of the time). Follow this road for about 1.5–2 miles as it swings west, then southwest, then north, and passes underneath the east faces of the Bridger Jack group, including Thumbelina and Sunflower Tower. Parking is where you choose it.

To reach North Six Shooter, continue on Hwy. 211 another 6.6 miles past the Beef Basin Road (just northwest of a concrete bridge and 28.5 miles from US 191), and make a sharp left onto the Davis Canyon Road. This road swings south, then west, toward North Six Shooter, and the drive is a matter of seeing how far your vehicle can go. Once the road gets too rough, it's time to walk.

69 SUPERCRACK BUTTRESS, SUPERCRACK

First ascent: Earl Wiggins, Ed Webster, and Bryan Becker, November 1976

Difficulty: I, 5.10+ for pitch 1; 5.11c for full climb

Time: 20 minutes for pitch 1; 2 hours for full climb

Equipment: Many #2–#3 Friends or Camalots for pitch 1; thinner gear (TCUs) for entire route

Steve Porcella on Supercrack, Indian Creek. © Cameron M. Burns.

Approach: From the road below the buttress, Supercrack—the most singular-looking crack system on the right (southwest) side of the buttress—can easily be located by standing on the downhill side of the sole cattle guard in the area. Line up the posts on either end of the cattle guard, and they point directly at Supercrack. It is only a short hike from the road up the hill to Supercrack Buttress.

Route: Pitch 1: Lay-back up the left side of a block sitting at the base of the route (5.10+), then climb the widening crack above to fixed anchors. Pitches 2–3: Continue up the crack. Pitch 2 is rated 5.10a. Pitch 3 is rated 5.11c.

Special considerations: Despite its reputation, the first pitch does vary somewhat, from thin hands at the bottom to wide hands/fists higher up. Be polite to other parties.

Descent: Most parties climb only the first pitch, then rappel off. From the top, make double-rope rappels down the route.

70 SUPERCRACK BUTTRESS, SUPERCORNER
First ascent: Unknown
Difficulty: I, 5.11d
Time: ½ hour
Equipment: Many #1 Friends or TCUs
Approach: From the road below the buttress, it is only a short hike up the hill

Supercrack Buttress: climb 73, The Wave; climb 72, Keyhole Flakes, climb 71, Coyne Crack; climb 70, Supercorner; climb 69, Supercrack. © Cameron M. Burns.

to Supercrack Buttress. Supercorner climbs the first right-facing corner about 40 feet to the left of Supercrack (climb 69).

Route: Pitch 1: Lay-back and stem up the corner for 60 feet to fixed anchors.

Descent: Make a single-rope rappel down the route.

71 SUPERCRACK BUTTRESS, COYNE CRACK

First ascent: Leonard Coyne, 1978
Difficulty: I, 5.12-
Time: ½ hour
Equipment: Many #1–#2 Friends
Approach: From the road below the buttress, it is only a short hike up the hill to Supercrack Buttress. Coyne Crack is the obvious, perfect splitter finger crack on the wall 20 feet to the left of Supercorner (climb 70).

Route: Pitch 1: Climb the thin crack for 80 feet to rappel anchors.

Special considerations: People with small hands find this route easier than 5.12-. Remarkably, many parties climb this crack using a lay-back. This is a popular top-rope route.

Descent: Make a single-rope rappel down the route.

72 SUPERCRACK BUTTRESS, KEYHOLE FLAKES

First ascent: Unknown
Difficulty: I, 5.10
Time: ½ hour
Equipment: Many #1–#2.5 Friends
Approach: From the road below the buttress, it is only a short hike up the hill to Supercrack Buttress. Keyhole Flakes follows a series of delicate flakes and cracks in the dark wall roughly 40 feet to the left of Coyne Crack (climb 71).

Route: Pitch 1: Climb the thin cracks and flakes for 70 feet to rappel anchors.

Special considerations: This route is better than it looks.

Descent: Make a rappel down the route.

73 SUPERCRACK BUTTRESS, THE WAVE

First ascent: Unknown
Difficulty: I, 5.10d
Time: ½ hour
Equipment: 3 sets of Friends, #1.5–#3
Approach: From the road below the buttress, it is only a short hike up the hill to Supercrack Buttress. About 50 feet to the left of Keyhole Flakes (climb 72) and roughly 150 feet to the left of Supercrack (climb 69) is a long, hourglass-shaped pillar leaning against the wall. The Wave climbs the left side of this pillar via a stunning hand crack.

Route: Pitch 1: Climb the crack to fixed anchors. There are many rest stances.

Special considerations: This is the best route on the buttress after Supercrack (climb 69).

Descent: Make a double-rope rappel from fixed anchors.

74 SUPERCRACK BUTTRESS, GORILLA CRACK

First ascent: Chip Chace and Steve Levin, 1978
Difficulty: I, 5.10b
Time: ½ hour
Equipment: 3 sets of Friends, #2–#3.5; 1 #1.5 Friend; 2 extra #3

Approach: From the road below the buttress, it is only a short hike up the hill to Supercrack Buttress. This route climbs a left-facing, rough-looking wall via a varying hand crack about 30 feet to the left of (and just around the next corner from) The Wave (climb 73).

Route: Pitch 1: Climb the crack to its top.
Special considerations: This route is easier than it's rated.
Descent: Make a double-rope rappel from fixed anchors.

75 SUPERCRACK BUTTRESS, INCREDIBLE HAND CRACK

First ascent: Rich Perch, John Bragg, Doug Snively, and Anne Tarver, 1978
Difficulty: I, 5.10c
Time: ½ hour

Supercrack Buttress: climb 76, Twin Cracks; climb 75, Incredible Hand Crack; climb 74, Gorilla Crack; climb 73, The Wave. © Cameron M. Burns.

Equipment: 7 #2.5 Friends; 1 #2 Friend; 1 #3 Friend

Approach: From the road below the buttress, it is only a short hike up the hill to Supercrack Buttress. The Incredible Hand Crack is about 60 feet left of Gorilla Crack (climb 74).

Route: Pitch 1: Climb the right side of a broken pillar to a ledge, then power up the steep, angling roof to the right.

Special considerations: This very popular route was originally called Sedimentary Journey.

Descent: Make a double-rope rappel from fixed anchors.

76 SUPERCRACK BUTTRESS, TWIN CRACKS

First ascent: Unknown

Difficulty: I, 5.8+

Time: ½ hour

Equipment: 1 set of camming units

Approach: From the road below the buttress, it is only a short hike up the hill to Supercrack Buttress. Start below the big right-facing dihedral roughly 100 feet to the left of Incredible Hand Crack (climb 75).

Route: Pitch 1: Climb a pair of cracks—one thin, one wide—to a two-bolt anchor.

Special considerations: This is one of the best beginner routes in the desert.

Descent: Make a single-rope rappel down the route.

77 THUMBELINA, LEARNING TO CRAWL

First ascent: Jeff Achey and Ed Webster, October 1, 1984

Difficulty: II, 5.11

Time: 3 hours

Equipment: 12 quickdraws

Approach: From the road, the towers are a short scramble up the hillside above. Thumbelina is the leftmost freestanding spire along the mesa, as viewed from the road. It's like a

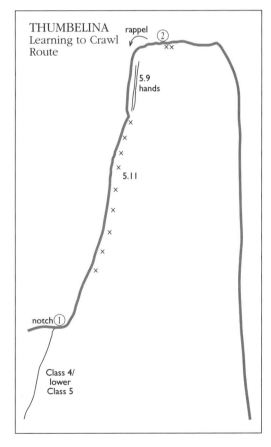

Bridger Jack Spire: climb 77, Thumbelina, Learning to Crawl; climb 78, Sunflower Tower, East Face. © Cameron M. Burns.

stout block, but with less-than-vertical sides; it's probably best described as a flat-topped pyramid. Learning to Crawl climbs the left edge of the stout block.

Route: Pitch 1: Climb Class 4/lower Class 5 terrain into the notch between Thumbelina and the formation to its left (south). Pitch 2: Climb the stunning bolt-protected face/arête to a 5.9 hand crack and the summit (5.11).

Descent: Rappel the route.

78 SUNFLOWER TOWER, EAST FACE

First ascent: Ed Webster and Alan Judish, May 14, 1984
Difficulty: III, 5.10
Time: ½ day
Equipment: 2 sets of Friends with extra #1–#3; 1 #3.5 Friend; 1 #4 Camalot; 1 set of TCUs; stoppers

Approach: From the road, the towers are a short scramble up the hillside above. The route starts up a thin crack on the east face, directly below the left side of the summit block.

Route: Pitch 1: Climb a thin hand crack over a bulging roof to a thin corner, which leads to a fixed belay. Pitch 2: Climb behind a flake left of the belay, and then climb a perfect hand crack up a left-facing corner to a belay just below the summit block. Pitch 3: Traverse to the right on unprotected ground and work around the top of the tower to a 5.8 corner leading to the summit.

Descent: Rappel the route.

79 NORTH SIX SHOOTER, LIGHTNING BOLT CRACKS

First ascent: Ed Webster and Pete Williams, April 1979
Difficulty: III, 5.11a
Time: ½ day
Equipment: 2 sets of Camalots with extra #1, #2, and #3; 1 set of TCUs; 1 set of wired stoppers
Approach: From where you parked on Davis Canyon Road, walk to the tower. The road dies out after a few miles, leaving most parties (depending on their vehicle

Steve Porcella on Lightning Bolt Cracks, North Six Shooter, Indian Creek.© Cameron M. Burns.

and driving style) with a roughly 45-minute to one-hour hike to the tower. This route starts up the first crack system from the right-hand edge of North Six Shooter's east face, but crosses over halfway up the tower to follow the left crack system on the summit tower.

Route: Pitch 1: Climb a finger crack (5.11a), then a thin hand crack as it widens

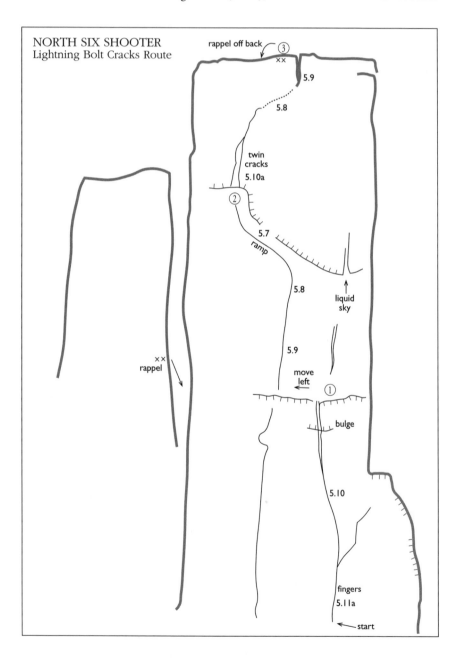

NORTH SIX SHOOTER
Lightning Bolt Cracks Route

rappel off back ③
xx

5.9

5.8

twin
cracks
5.10a

②

5.7
ramp

5.8

liquid
sky

5.9

xx
rappel

move
left
①

bulge

5.10

fingers
5.11a

start

up over a bulge to a fixed belay. Pitch 2: Move left (don't go straight, up into Liquid Sky's scary off-width roof above the belay), and climb a left-angling ramp under a large roof to a belay at the edge of the roof (5.7). Pitch 3: Mantle the roof (5.10a) and follow the crack system to the summit.

Climb 79, North Six Shooter, Lightning Bolt Cracks. © Cameron M. Burns.

Special considerations: Only the first few feet of this route are 5.11. Lots of folks yard through them. This route gets lots of traffic.

Descent: Make two double-rope rappels down the west face (on the opposite side of the tower from the route), using fixed anchors.

TEXAS CANYON

Texas Canyon is a wildly remote area of spires, buttes, and mesas in the very southeastern corner of Utah. It is easily one of the most beautiful areas in the desert southwest, and almost unexplored by climbers. (Don't tell anyone, okay?)

Rock climbs in Texas Canyon are true wilderness experiences that require hard driving, long approaches, and difficult, sometimes scary, climbing. But just a single visit to Texas Canyon will impress upon you just how isolated and beautiful portions of the Colorado Plateau can be.

The two routes that are described in this chapter—the South Face on Texas Tower and Creatures from the Black Saloon on Lone Star—represent something of the extremes that can be found in Texas Canyon. One is an extremely demanding free-climb; the other is a fairly straightforward jaunt up a thin but elegant spire. Enjoy!

Area climbing regulations: The canyon lies in public land managed by the Bureau of Land Management (BLM) or the U.S. Forest Service; there are no climbing regulations, although it is up to all climbers to leave as little impact as possible so that this policy remains.

Special considerations: Do not disturb archaeological ruins, if you should find any.

Getting there: There are two ways to reach Texas Canyon: by driving in or by rappelling in (the more preferred route). For both options, start in Blanding on US 191 and drive about 4 miles south of town, then turn right (at a Shell gas station) onto Hwy. 95. Follow Hwy. 95 for exactly 15.4 miles to an unnamed, unmarked dirt road leading off to the right. About the only way to tell you're at the right road is to measure mileage from the intersection of Hwy. 95 and US 191, back near the gas station. Here the two ways to Texas Canyon diverge.

To drive in, take the dirt road to the right, which leads up the bottom of Arch Canyon, for roughly an hour and a half (the mileage is probably about 9 miles) until its end. This road is extremely rough and four-wheel drive is required. The road crosses the streambed many times in an area that has been recommended for wilderness protection; so to limit damage to the canyon, I advise folks to rappel in from the canyon top instead.

To rappel in, continue on Hwy. 95 past the dirt-road turnoff for the four-wheel-drive route, to Texas Flat Road (San Juan County Rd. 263, which is just west of mile marker 108), then turn right. Follow Texas Flat Road for about 6.8 miles to a campground and overlook on the right. Texas Tower is obvious in the canyon below. Rappel into the canyon using trees as anchors. (Bring two ropes to leave in place.) Scrambling leads to a campsite at the junction of Arch and Texas Canyons.

80 TEXAS TOWER, SOUTH FACE

First ascents: Tim Toula and Kathy Zaiser, April 1987. *First free ascent:* Bret Ruckman and Tim Coats, October 1991.

Difficulty: IV, 5.11c or 5.10, C1

Time: 1 full day

Equipment: 3 sets of Camalots through #5; 2 #4 Big Bro tube chocks or equivalent; wired stoppers

Approach: From the campsite at the end of the road, regardless whether you drove or rappelled here, there are two canyons to the west: Arch Canyon to the right (northwest) and Texas Canyon to the left (west). Hike up Texas Canyon roughly a mile, and Texas Tower becomes obvious on the right (north) side of the drainage. It's a huge, yellow tower. The South Face route climbs the obvious splitter crack that stretches from bottom to top of the tower's south face.

Route: Pitch 1: Start in a left-facing corner (loose) and climb to a decent ledge with fixed anchors (5.9). Pitch 2: Continue up an off-width chimney to a small roof, then a belay stance with fixed anchors (5.9+). Pitch 3: Climb a difficult, frustrating chimney to a small roof, then to a single-bolt belay (5.10). Pitch 4: Continue straight up in a broken corner past a death block and some face-climbing (5.10 R) to a ledge with fixed anchors (5.10). Pitch 5: Continue up a wide (5–8 inches) off-width past several bolts to an exposed belay stance with fixed anchors, (5.11c or 5.10, C1). Pitch 6: Begin with a squeeze, then a wild and scary chimney to a single-bolt belay (5.10). Pitch 7: Continue up the chimney, passing some fixed gear to a decent belay (a fixed anchor) on the summit's shoulder (5.10). Pitch 8: Climb to the top (5.10+).

Special considerations: This is a scary and wild climb requiring many large pieces of gear for off-width and chimney climbing. Bring whatever you can get your hands on, plus 200-foot ropes.

Descent: Rappel the west side of the tower (left side, when viewed from below the South Face) on double ropes. After two rappels, finding the third is

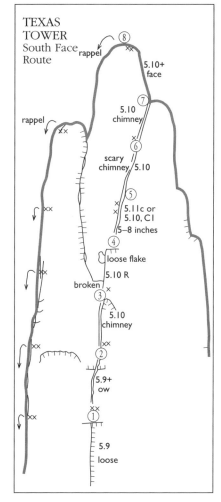

TEXAS TOWER
South Face Route

rappel

8
5.10+ face

7
5.10 chimney

rappel

6
scary chimney / 5.10

5
5.11c or 5.10, C1
5–8 inches

4
loose flake
5.10 R

broken
3
5.10 chimney

2
5.9+ ow

1
5.9 loose

Jon Butler jugging on Creatures from the Black Saloon, Lone Star, Texas Canyon.
© Cameron M. Burns.

tricky. Walk west along an exposed ramp (while still tied in) until you can find the anchors. The last rappel does not quite reach the ground with regular 165-foot ropes. Finish the rappel on a stance, then down-climb to the base of the route.

81 LONE STAR, CREATURES FROM THE BLACK SALOON

First ascent: Jon Butler, Jesse Harvey, and Cameron Burns, November 1996
Difficulty: I, 5.7, A1
Time: 1 full day
Equipment: 2 sets of Friends with 4 #3.5 Friends; 1 set of TCUs; 1 #4 Camalot; 1 set wired stoppers; 6 knifeblades; 6 Lost Arrows (thin to medium); 10 angles between ½–1 inch; several Birdbeaks; many bolt hangers ¼ inch or ⅜ inch or tie-offs for bolt studs
Approach: From the campsite at the end of the road, regardless whether you

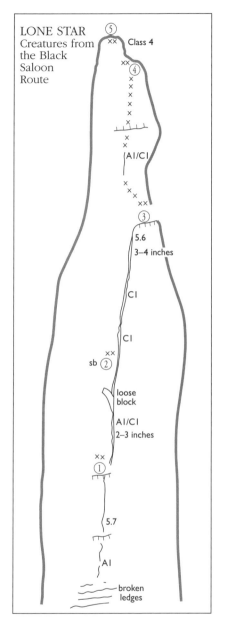

LONE STAR
Creatures from the Black Saloon Route

⑤ xx Class 4

xx
④
x
x
x
x
x
x
x
x
A1/C1
x
x x
x
xx
③
5.6
3–4 inches

C1

C1

xx
sb ②

loose block

A1/C1
2–3 inches

xx
①

5.7

A1

broken ledges

Creatures from the Black Saloon, Lone Star, Texas Canyon. © Cameron M. Burns.

drove or rappelled here, there are two canyons to the west: Arch Canyon to the right (northwest) and Texas Canyon to the left (west). Hike up Texas Canyon roughly a mile, and Texas Tower becomes obvious on the right (north) side of the drainage. Lone Star sits just 400 feet to Texas Tower's left (west), and at first appears to be part of the canyon wall until you hike up to its base. It is obvious from Texas Tower's south face. Creatures from the Black Saloon climbs a low-angled ramp on the south face of the tower, before joining a crack/corner system on the east side.

Route: Pitch 1: Begin A1 and climb past an expanding flake. Continue to a belay ledge (5.7). Pitch 2: Pass several bolts and climb A1/C1 up loose rock, passing a death block to a hanging belay on the left wall. Pitch 3: Continue up the widening crack (C1), then climb 5.6 to fixed anchors on a ledge. Pitch 4: Climb a short bolt ladder to a crack, aid up the crack (A1, C1), then follow a bolt ladder to the summit shoulder and fixed anchors. Pitch 5: Scramble to the summit.

Special considerations: This route is very casual compared to Texas Tower. Portions of the route can be done free. It will likely go clean very easily.

Descent: Rappel the route. A rope between the tops of pitches 3 and 4 helps one pull into the pitch 3 belay on the descent.

COMB RIDGE

Comb Ridge is a long, angular ridge cutting across the very southeastern corner of Utah. While there have only been a handful of routes developed here, Magic Man on The Prayer Stick is as classic as any route in this guidebook. The Prayer Stick is a stunning tower/pillar leaning against Comb Ridge southwest of Bluff.

Area climbing regulations: Comb Ridge lies on public land, managed by the Bureau of Land Management (BLM). There are no restrictions on climbing at present, although it is up to all climbers to leave as little impact as possible so that this policy remains.

Special considerations: This is likely the first route on Comb Ridge to be described in any guidebook. Climbers who visit the area and develop routes here should be extremely conscientious when it comes to their impact.

Getting there: From Bluff on US 191, go west on US 163, and in about 8 miles Comb Ridge is evident, stretching away to the north (right). At 8.5 miles from Bluff, reach San Juan County Rd. 235 and turn north onto it. Follow San Juan County Rd. 235 north for 3 miles, and The Prayer Stick is obvious on the right (east). Park along the road.

82 THE PRAYER STICK, MAGIC MAN

First ascents: Mike Baker and Leslie Henderson, March 1997. *First free ascent:* Mike Baker and Chris Ducker, April 1997.

Difficulty: III, 5.10+

Time: ½ day

Equipment: 1 set of Camalots to #5, with 2 extra #3 and #4; 1 set of TCUs

Approach: From where you parked, walk up to the tower. The hike takes 30 minutes. Magic Man follows the crack system on the right side of the tower.

Route: Pitch 1: Begin up a right-facing corner to a belay ledge at fixed anchors (5.7). Pitch 2: Climb a 5.10+ lay-back to a natural-gear belay at a stance. Pitch 3: Continue up the corner and climb to the right, around a roof, to a cave and another

THE PRAYER STICK
Magic Man Route

⑤

scramble to top

④ ××
rappel

5.8

cave ③ no fixed anchors

×
5.8
5.9
×

② no fixed anchors

5.10+
lay-back

××
①
5.7

loose

natural-gear belay (5.9). Pitch 4: Continue up the crack/corner system to a fixed-anchor belay (5.8). Pitch 5: Scramble 30 feet to the top.

Descent: Make double-rope rappels down the route from the top of pitch 4.

The Prayer Stick, Comb Ridge. Magic Man climbs the right side of the pillar. © Cameron M. Burns.

VALLEY OF THE GODS

Valley of the Gods is not really a valley, but a remote area of dry washes and draws, spires, buttes, and mesas in the very southeastern corner of Utah.

It is one of the southwest's hidden climbing gems. Similar in layout and feel to Monument Valley, Valley of the Gods lies just 20 miles north of the former on land managed by the Bureau of Land Management (BLM), and is thus open to climbing (unlike Monument Valley itself, where climbing is "discouraged"). In essence, it is something of a "white man's" Monument Valley.

Stories about climbing in Valley of the Gods have filtered back to desert climbers ever since Eric Bjørnstad and Ron Wiggle's historic first visit in 1974, but the stories have always described poor protection, horrifyingly loose rock, and huge approaches. Certainly, some of those elements exist, but the essence of Valley of the Gods has been missed. The place is a fabulous collection of towers and buttes in a rather compact setting, not unlike Arches National Park. And, like Arches, the climbs here vary from short, free routes to big aid affairs taking a full rack and a long day.

The big difference, however, is that if you visit Valley of the Gods to climb, you're likely to have the entire place to yourself. To quote desert pioneer Todd Gordon, "Such insane towers and no people; just the coyote, spider, snake, and buzzard to watch the heroics of these crags. I like this place." (*Climbing,* April 1984, No. 83.)

Area climbing regulations: The routes in Valley of the Gods lie on public land, managed by the BLM. There are no restrictions on climbing at present, although it is up to all climbers to leave as little impact as possible so that this policy remains.

Special considerations: The rock in Valley of the Gods is generally very good, but can be "Entrada-like" in some places. The rock boasts very pronounced, thick layers (usually 100 feet or so), and the thin bands of crud that separate these layers provide most of the Valley's excitement. The talus cones are extremely loose soil and the area is notoriously dusty.

Getting there: The eastern end of the Valley of the Gods Loop Road (San Juan County Rd. 242, though unmarked as such) lies exactly 8.1 miles north of the town of Mexican Hat, which is on the northwest side of US 163. If you are coming from the north, it is exactly 18 miles southeast of the post office in Bluff, on the corner of Fifth East Street. There is a huge sign alongside US 163, pointing down the Valley of the Gods Loop Road. This guidebook describes the towers' location by using odometer readings from the loop road's intersection with US 163. The loop road ends on Hwy. 261.

Mileage	Formation
0.0	US 163
3.1	The Anvil is on the left.
3.6	Petard Tower is on the left.
7.9	North Tower and Arrowhead Spire are on the right; Eagle Plume Tower is on the left, with its north face facing the road.

8.2   Tom Tom Tower (a big mesa with multiple summits) is on the right. On the ridge behind Tom Tom Tower is a squat, square, short tower called Tides of Mind.

8.7   Putterman on the Throne and Putterman in a Bathtub are the twin buttes on the right; Eagle Plume Tower is on the left, with its south face facing the road.

9.7   Two buttes are on the right; The Hand of Puttima is the one farthest (west) from the road.

83 PETARD TOWER (A.K.A. PRAIRIE DOG ON A MOUND), HURLEY-REARICK ROUTE

First ascents: George Hurley and Dave Rearick, May 1977. *First-pitch variation:* Cameron Burns, Jon Butler, Jesse "The Body" Harvey, and Lefty Angus Burns, January 1999.

Difficulty: II, 5.10- or 5.9, C1

Time: ½ day

Equipment: 1 set of Friends with a #5 Camalot for pitch 2; 1 set of TCUs

Approach: From 3.6 miles along Valley of the Gods Loop Road, walk up the southeast (left) side of the mesa on which Petard Tower sits, then move to the right, around the tower to the northeast (road) side of the tower. There are two obvious crack systems on this face. The right crack is a wide, rotten chimney filled with bird dung and debris. This is the start of the original Hurley-Rearick Route.

Route: Pitch 1: Climb the nasty chimney to the first prominent ledge system (5.9 R). It's advisable to move the belay right 40 feet on the prominent ledge. Pitch 2: Move to the right on the ledge system 40 feet, and climb the right side of a prominent block sitting against the

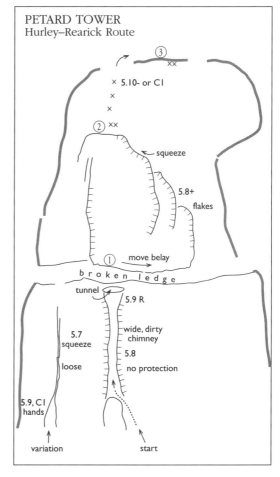

PETARD TOWER
Hurley–Rearick Route

Northeast face of Petard Tower, showing climb 83 and the variation to pitch 1 (83a).
© Cameron M. Burns.

northeast face of the tower (5.8+), past flakes and edges, squeezing through a wide crack to reach the top of the block. Walk left, to a fixed anchor. Pitch 3: Climb the bolt ladder (5.10- or C1) to the summit.

Special considerations: There is a variation to pitch 1, roughly 50 feet to the left of the dirty chimney, that climbs the left-hand of two cracks that form an upside-down Y (5.9, C1). It's much easier to protect. The Hurley-Rearick Route gets much better after the low-quality first pitch. There are no fixed anchors atop the first pitch. There is much loose rock.

Descent: Rappel the route.

84 NORTH TOWER, NORTHEAST ROUTE

First ascent: Brian Povolny and Will Taylor, 1983
Difficulty: II, 5.10+ or C1
Time: 1 full day
Equipment: 2 sets of camming units with extra hand- to fist-sized pieces; TCUs; stoppers

Approach: At 7.9 miles along the Valley of the Gods Loop Road, there is a pullout on the north side of the road, below the north face of Eagle Plume Tower. Park here and hike to the North Tower, then around the back (north face) of the tower, which is much shorter than the front (south face). The Northeast Route becomes obvious; it is the incredible splitter crack system near the left end of the north face.

Route: Pitch 1: Follow the splitter crack system (there are two options to start, then move into the left-hand wide crack), which leads to a huge ledge (5.10+ or C1). Pitch 2: Climb up and left into the obvious corner system to the east summit (5.9).

Special considerations: Several variations are possible on pitch 2.

Descent: Rappel the route.

85 ARROWHEAD SPIRE, SOUTHEAST FACE

First ascent: Jeff Widen and Rich McDonald, April 1994

Difficulty: I, 5.9, A2

Time: ½ day

Equipment: 2 set of Friends, with several extra #3.5 and #4; 3 #4 Camalots; 2 #5 Camalots; 3 knifeblades

Approach: At 7.9 miles along the Valley of the Gods Loop Road, there is a pullout on the north side of the road, below the north face of Eagle Plume Tower. Park here and hike to the North Tower, then around to the back (north face) of the

Arrowhead Spire, North Tower from the north, Valley of the Gods, Utah.
© Cameron M. Burns.

tower. When below the North-east Route (climb 84) on North Tower, walk left (east) toward Arrowhead Spire, the spectacular 100-foot-tall freestanding pinnacle sitting on the same ridge as North Tower. The route climbs the south face (the front), via a wide crack system that goes out over a stunning roof.

Route: Pitch 1: Begin up the obvious crack under the roof; the crack gets wider as it crests the roof. Climb out the roof using #4 Camalots, and belay at two bolts (C2). Pitch 2: Climb past several bolts and up to a ledge with a fixed anchor (5.9, A2). Pitch 3: Climb easy ground to the summit.

Special considerations: Leap-frogging the wide gear helps, but can be scary. This route should go clean on its next ascent, and will likely go free.

Descent: Rappel into the notch between North Tower and Arrowhead Spire.

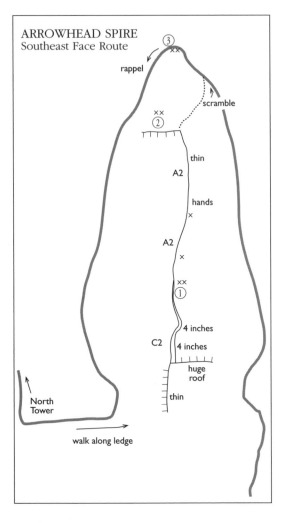

86 TIDES OF MIND, NORTH FACE

First ascents: Jeff Cristol, December 1989. *First free ascent:* Keen Butterworth and George Arms, July 1990.

Difficulty: II, 5.11+ or 5.9, C1

Time: ½ day

Equipment: 2 sets of Friends, with several extra #2–#3

Approach: At 7.9 miles along the Valley of the Gods Loop Road, there is a pullout on the north side of the road, below the north face of Eagle Plume Tower. Walk west, along the large valley between Tom Tom Tower and North Tower. Tides of Mind is obvious on the ridge left (south) of the valley.

Route: Pitch 1: Climb the lone splitter crack system on the north face of the tower (5.11+ or 5.9, C1), then scramble to the top.

Descent: Rappel the route.

Tides of Mind, Valley of the Gods, Utah. © Cameron M. Burns.

87 EAGLE PLUME TOWER, SOUTH FACE

First ascents: Bill Forrest and Frank Lupton, 1976. *First free ascent:*
Craig Kenyon and Jeff Cristol, December 1989.
Difficulty: III, 5.10
Time: 1 full day
Equipment: 2 sets of camming units to #4 Camalot; TCUs; 1 set of
wired stoppers

Approach: At 8.7 miles along the Valley of the Gods Loop Road, Eagle Plume
Tower is on the left, with its south face facing the road. The South Face route climbs
the prominent crack system in the center of the south face.

Route: Pitch 1: Climb through some loose, rotten rock and stair-step up and
left onto the huge ledge coming in from the left (5.8). Pitch 2: Climb the obvious
crack system above the ledge, past three horizontal rock bands, then a finger crack
(5.10) leading to a belay at a sloping stance at the base of two cracks. Pitch 3: Climb
the right-hand of two cracks above the ledge (the S crack) for a full rope length of
mostly hands (5.9) and finish by climbing through a thin, rotten band that leads to
a ledge. Belay at a large block with a calcite covering. Pitch 4: Move left, and climb
the large, obvious, right-facing corner above the ledge (5.9) via a hand crack. From
the top of the fourth pitch, scramble to the summit.

Special considerations: This route has some loose rock.
Descent: Rappel the route.

Climb 87, Eagle Plume Tower, South Face. © Cameron M. Burns.

88 PUTTERMAN ON THE THRONE, SUPERCALIFRAGILISTIC-EXPIALIPUTTERMAN

First ascent: Jesse "The Body" Harvey, Cameron Burns, and Lefty Angus Burns, January 1999
Difficulty: III, 5.9, C1
Time: ½ day
Equipment: 2 sets of camming units to #5 Camalot, with extra #2–#4 Camalots; 1 set of TCUs

Approach: At 8.7 miles along Valley of the Gods Loop Road, Putterman on the Throne and Putterman in a Bathtub are the twin buttes on the right. Both Supercalifragilisticexpialiputterman and It's a Mad, Mad, Mad, Mad Putterman (climb 89) begin from the notch between the two towers. To reach the notch, start at the far western end of the mesa on which the towers sit, which is a 20-minute hike from the road. Scramble (Class 4) up onto the mesa's end, and walk east along a large ledge system on the north side of the tower to the notch between the two. To reach Supercalifragilisticexpialiputterman, climb up into the notch from the ledge (5.9) and then walk west (back the direction you came) to the first splitter crack on the south face of Putterman on the Throne. This crack is the first pitch of Supercalifragilisticexpialiputterman.

Route: Pitch 1: Climb the splitter crack (5.9, C1, but will go free) to a large ledge and three-bolt anchor. Pitch 2: Climb the bulge on the ridge, then a short bolt ladder (C1) through steep, very soft rock to another large ledge with a two-bolt anchor. Pitch 3: Continue up the ridge. Climb a 5.8 bulge protected by a bolt, then a band of loose brown rock, then scramble to the top to a three-bolt anchor.

Descent: Rappel the route.

Jesse Harvey following pitch 3, Supercalifragilisticexpialiputterman, Putterman on the Throne, Valley of the Gods, Utah. © Cameron M. Burns.

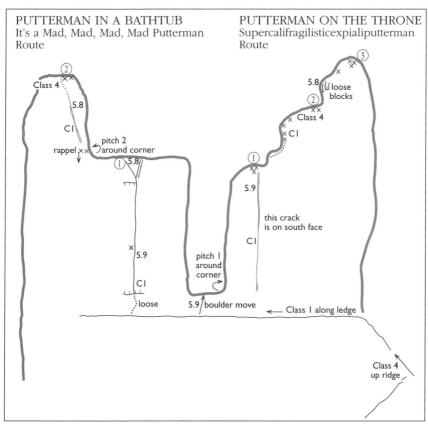

PUTTERMAN IN A BATHTUB
It's a Mad, Mad, Mad, Mad Putterman Route

PUTTERMAN ON THE THRONE
Supercalifragilisticexpialiputterman Route

89 PUTTERMAN IN A BATHTUB, IT'S A MAD, MAD, MAD, MAD PUTTERMAN

First ascent: Cameron Burns, Jesse "The Body" Harvey, Jon Butler, and Lefty Angus Burns, January 1999
Difficulty: II, 5.9, C1
Time: ½ day
Equipment: 2 sets of camming units to #5 Camalot, with extra #2–#5 Camalots; 1 set of TCUs or equivalent

Approach: At 8.7 miles along Valley of the Gods Loop Road, Putterman on the Throne and Putterman in a Bathtub are the twin buttes on the right. Both Supercalifragilisticexpialiputterman (climb 88) and It's a Mad, Mad, Mad, Mad Putterman

Putterman on the Throne and Putterman in a Bathtub, Valley of the Gods, Utah.
© Cameron M. Burns.

begin from the notch between the two towers. To reach the notch, start at the far western end of the mesa on which the towers sit, which is a 20-minute hike from the road. Scramble (Class 4) up onto the mesa's end, and walk east along a large ledge system on the north side of the tower to the notch between the two. To reach It's a Mad, Mad, Mad, Mad Putterman, continue walking east to a prominent splitter crack with a bolt next to it 50 feet up. The crack is the first pitch of It's a Mad, Mad, Mad, Mad Putterman.

Route: Pitch 1: Scramble through a loose band to the base of the splitter, and climb it to a ledge (5.9, C1). Move left on the ledge and follow a thin crack that diagonals up and left to a huge gravelly ledge on the crest of the ridge. Pitch 2: Move to the right, around the tower onto the southwest side, and climb the obvious corner to the top (C1, 5.8).

Special considerations: This route will go free.

Descent: Rappel the route.

90 THE HAND OF PUTTIMA, JUST AN OLD-FASHIONED PUTT SONG

First ascent: Cameron "Wigfoot" Burns, Benny "I'm" Bach, and Lefty Angus Burns, March 1999

Difficulty: II, 5.9, C1

Time: ½ day

Equipment: 2 sets of camming units to #5 Camalot, with extra hand/fist size; 1 set of TCUs; 1 set of stoppers; 6 pitons from knifeblades to ⅝ angles

Approach: At 9.7 miles along Valley of the Gods Loop Road, the road crosses a wash (just south of Putterman in a Bathtub). There are two buttes on the right side of the road. The Hand of Puttima is the butte farthest west (farthest from the road). Park near the wash, and hike to the north face of the formation. The walk takes ½ hour. Just an Old-Fashioned Putt Song starts on the far right (west) end of the north face.

Route: Pitch 1: Nail thin cracks that lead to a wide, right-to-left-angling crack (A1), then climb the angling crack to a stance (5.8, C1). From the stance, move up

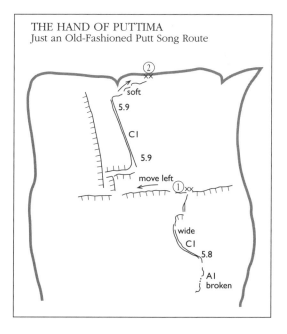

THE HAND OF PUTTIMA
Just an Old-Fashioned Putt Song Route

Above: *Climb 90, The Hand of Puttima, Just an Old-Fashioned Putt Song.* Photo by Benny Bach. Left: *Benny Bach on pitch 1, Just an Old-Fashioned Putt Song, The Hand of Puttima, Valley of the Gods, Utah.* © Cameron M. Burns.

and right to a huge ledge and a two-bolt anchor. Pitch 2: Move left on the ledge to a prominent fist crack with several bolts below it. From below the crack, move left 40 feet, climb a short corner (C1, 5.9), then move back right, to the first crack. Climb it to the top (5.9, C1), then move right, up soft ledges to the summit anchors.

Descent: Rappel the route.

MEXICAN HAT

Mexican Hat is more an oddity than a climb. But it's a really cool oddity and, hence, is included here. Mexican Hat is literally a big, concave disc of sandstone sitting atop a really small base. The first ascent of the formation was made by Royal Robbins and Jack Turner in 1962. In 1981, Banditos climbing gang members Stan Mish and Dan Langmade took a look at the Robbins Route and decided it was too scary. They then created their own route up the south side of the hat, placing a half dozen or so bolts and creating the modern, very easy, classic "route."

Area climbing regulations: Mexican Hat lies on public land, managed by the

Jesse Harvey and Jon Butler on Bandito Route, Mexican Hat. © Cameron M. Burns.

Bureau of Land Management (BLM). There are no restrictions on climbing at present, although it is up to all climbers to leave as little impact as possible so that this policy remains.

Special considerations: The Navajo occasionally use Mexican Hat for special ceremonies (most of which aren't religious). While it is totally legal to climb Mexican Hat, be polite and courteous.

Getting there: From the town of Mexican Hat, Utah, Mexican Hat (the rock) is 2 miles north on US 163, on the right (east) side of the road. From the north (Blanding or Bluff) via US 191, go south and then east on US 163; Mexican Hat (the rock) is exactly 24.1 miles from Fifth East Street (the location of the new post office) in Bluff.

There is a huge sign on the side of the road announcing Mexican Hat's location. Turn east onto the unmarked dirt road, and drive around the south side of the mesa on top of which Mexican Hat sits. It's best to park on the far eastern side of the formation.

91 MEXICAN HAT, BANDITO ROUTE

First ascent: Stan Mish and Dan Langmade, 1981
Difficulty: I, C1
Time: 5 minutes
Equipment: 7 quickdraws
Approach: From where you parked, walk up the east side of the mesa on which Mexican Hat sits. The Bandito Route lies on the south side of the hat's brim.
Route: Pitch 1: Clip the five bolts that lead to the top (C1).
Special considerations: The first bolt requires either an 8-foot-tall climber to clip it, or someone to get down on all fours doggy-style and give the leader another 2 feet of elevation.
Descent: Rappel the route.

CENTRAL UTAH

SAN RAFAEL SWELL

The San Rafael Swell is one of the greatest wilderness regions of the American West. It is a stunning place of striking pinnacles, huge buttes (many still unclimbed), and wide, deep, sprawling canyons. Although the Swell has been visited by climbers for decades, only a handful of routes were established here until the early 1990s, when Salt Lake City climbers began actively climbing all the major formations and exploring the surrounding canyons' walls. The number of routes now established in the Swell is likely approaching (or may have exceeded) 1,000.

The collection of routes described herein is by no means comprehensive: It represents just a smattering of the vast variety of climbing opportunities that can be found in the Swell, from big-wall/aid-type routes to short, moderate rock climbs to exploratory routes that verge on mountaineering. If you like remote areas with almost no other climbers, the Swell is for you.

Area regulations: The routes in the San Rafael Swell lie on public land, managed by the Bureau of Land Management (BLM). There are no restrictions on climbing at present, although it is up to all climbers to leave as little impact as possible so that this policy remains.

Special considerations: The rock in the southern Swell seems to be somewhat softer than the rock in the northern part of the Swell. Two-wheel-drive vehicles can make it to every climb in the Swell that is included in this volume. The roads are very good.

Getting to the Northern San Rafael Swell: For climbing routes in the Northern San Rafael Swell, it is easiest to base oneself at the San Rafael Campground on the San Rafael River. From I-70 take exit 129 north and follow this road for 20.8 miles. The road starts out paralleling I-70 for several miles before swinging north. Just past the turnoff to the right (east) into the campground is a bridge over the river.

To reach Buckhorn Wash north of the river, reset your odometer at this bridge. At 0.8 mile is The Lightbulb (a.k.a. James' Tower). At 1.3 miles is the Wisdom Tooth, up the first drainage northwest of The Lightbulb. At 4.3 miles pass an outstanding petroglyph panel that is worth a look. At 7.8 miles is Scenic Byway on the left (west) side of the road.

To reach Bottleneck Peak and Window Blind Peak drive south from the bridge, back toward I-70. Take the first right, 0.8 mile south of the bridge (roughly 20 miles from I-70), and Bottleneck Peak is the obvious butte high on a ridge to the south. Park wherever looks the closest and hike south to the butte. For Window Blind Peak, continue south on the road leading back to I-70. Window Blind Peak is the highest, biggest formation off to the east. Park anywhere along the road south of Bottleneck Peak that looks nearest to the long hike to Window Blind Peak.

Getting to the Southern San Rafael Swell: From I-70 take exit 129 and drive south. The dirt road swings west and parallels I-70 for several miles before heading south again. When you are 5.6 miles south of I-70, pass the Head of Sinbad Road. Go straight for another 5.4 miles (11 miles from I-70) to the Reds Canyon/Tan Seep Road, and turn right (southwest). Follow this road for 4 miles to a **T** intersection, and turn right (west). Follow this road for another 2.1 miles to an intersection with an unnamed road, best identified by a large sign warning about the hazards of old mines.

To reach Family Butte, drive another 0.7 mile straight past the mine warning sign, and park along the side of the road. Getting to Family Butte (the obvious five-summitted mesa to the west) requires hiking a mile. To reach Turkey Tower, take the unnamed road leading northwest from the mine warning sign. Follow this unnamed road for 3.3 miles as it winds around onto the mesa upon which Turkey Tower sits, and passes within 0.5 mile of the tower itself.

It is also possible to reach Family Butte and Turkey Tower by exiting from I-70 on Hwy. 24 and driving 26 miles south to the Goblin Valley Road. Turn west, and follow this road for 12 miles to the Family Butte area.

NORTHERN SAN RAFAEL SWELL

92 UNNAMED MESA, BAD OBSESSION

First ascent: Mike Friedrichs and Gene Roush, October 1991
Difficulty: III, 5.11d
Time: 1 full day
Equipment: 3 sets of camming units; 2 sets of TCUs

Climb 92, Unnamed Mesa, Bad Obsession. © Cameron M. Burns.

Approach: It is a 30-minute hike northwest from the San Rafael Campground and bridge over the San Rafael River to an unnamed mesa. Look for a light brown area of broken rock on the mesa's northeast side or the right side of the most prominent pillar sitting against the mesa. Bad Obsession climbs a difficult-to-locate splitter crack system (and rap slings) just left of the area of broken rock.

Route: Pitch 1: Climb a thin corner to an overhanging finger crack, then a wider crack above. The pitch ends at a two-bolt belay (5.11d). Pitch 2: Climb a hand crack up a stunning corner (5.10-) to fixed anchors. Pitch 3: Class 4 scrambling leads to the top of the buttress.

Descent: Rappel the route.

93 ASSEMBLY HALL PEAK, POSTCARD OF THE HANGING

First ascent: James Garrett and Kris Pietryga, April 1998
Difficulty: III, 5.10, C1
Time: 1 full day
Equipment: 2 sets of Camalots

Approach: Assembly Hall Peak is the large butte lying just southeast of the San Rafael Campground. It is best approached as a hike from the campground. The hike takes 45 minutes to an hour. Postcard of the Hanging climbs an obvious corner on

Climb 93, Assembly Hall Peak, Postcard of the Hanging. © Cameron M. Burns.

the northeast face, just around the corner to the left (east) of the side that is visible from the campground.

Route: Pitch 1: Climb a left-facing corner hands to fists, then climb around some bolt-protected flakes, then back into a nice hand and fist crack to a ledge and two-bolt belay (5.10, C1). Pitch 2: Climb some face moves a half pitch to a ledge and an obvious traverse. Pitch 3: Traverse far to the right into a large bowl, then climb easy ground to a left-facing dihedral with several bolts. Climb it to the top.

Special considerations: The route will likely go free.

Descent: Rappel the northeast face.

94 THE LIGHTBULB (A.K.A. JAMES' TOWER), ORIGINAL ROUTE

First ascent: James Garrett, April 25, 1990

Difficulty: II, 5.10, C1

Time: ½ day

Equipment: 2 sets of camming units, with several large units

Approach: Climbing up to the base of the tower is the crux. There are several alternatives that are obvious from the Buckhorn Wash Road. The route begins on the north side of the tower, and wraps around it.

Route: Pitch 1: Starting on the north side of the tower, climb the ever-widening crack as it moves clockwise around the tower (5.10). Pitch 2: Aid the bolt ladder above to the summit (C1).

Special considerations: Many parties do the route in three pitches with a belay halfway up the first pitch, where the crack becomes horizontal for a few feet.

Descent: Make a double-rope rappel off the east side of the tower, using 200-foot ropes.

Climb 94, The Lightbulb, Original Route. © Cameron M. Burns.

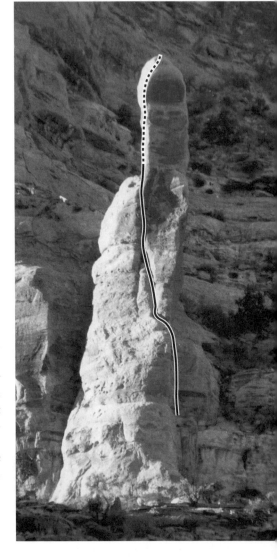

95 WISDOM TOOTH, CRYPTOGAMIC FOREST

First ascent: Mike Freidrichs and George Jamison, 1990 (pitch 1);
Dave Medara and John Merriam, 1996 (pitch 2)
Difficulty: II, 5.11-
Time: ½ day
Equipment: 2 sets of camming units
Approach: Hike west up the first drainage northwest of The Lightbulb to Wisdom Tooth. Cryptogamic Forest climbs the obvious splitter crack that splits the north side of the tower.
Route: Pitch 1: Climb the ever-widening crack to fixed anchors (5.11b). Pitch 2: Continue up a wide crack to the summit (5.9).
Descent: Rappel the route.

96 BUCKHORN WASH, SCENIC BYWAY

First ascent: James Garrett and Franziska Garrett, 1992
Difficulty: II, 5.10
Time: 3 hours
Equipment: 1 set of TCUs; 1 set of camming units; a piece of wide gear (#5 Camalot) for pitch 2
Approach: Scenic Byway is on the west side of Buckhorn Wash Road, 7.8 miles from the bridge.
Route: Pitch 1: Climb the stunning hand crack to a two-bolt belay. Pitch 2: Climb a funky off-width above the belay (5.10) in the right-facing corner to a bolt, then immediately traverse left. (Don't move to the right, to the belay anchors atop Metacarpal Road Map). Continue up easy ground to a belay ledge. Pitch 3: Continue up and to the right (5.7) to another fixed belay. Pitch 4:

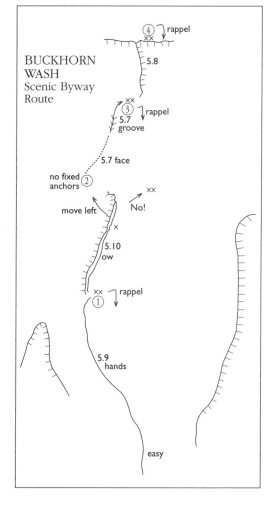

BUCKHORN
WASH
Scenic Byway
Route

4 rappel
5.8
3 rappel
5.7 groove
5.7 face
no fixed anchors 2
move left
No!
5.10 ow
1 rappel
5.9 hands
easy

Climb 96, Buckhorn Wash, Scenic Byway. © Cameron M. Burns.

Traverse right and climb a left-facing dihedral (5.8) to fixed anchors at the top of the mesa.

Special considerations: Many parties do only the first pitch, then rap off to avoid the off-width (pitch 2). Pitches 3 and 4 are also excellent.

Descent: Rappel the route.

97 BOTTLENECK PEAK, WOODY'S ROOFS

First ascent: James Garrett and Dave Medara, November 18, 1992
Difficulty: IV, 5.10, A2
Time: 1 full day

The four pitches of climb 97, Bottleneck Peak, Woody's Roofs. © Cameron M. Burns.

Equipment: 3 sets of camming units to #4; 3 #5 Camalots; 2 sets of TCUs; 1 set of stoppers; 1 set of RPs; a selection of 15 pitons from ½ inch down to Birdbeaks

Approach: Bottleneck Peak is the obvious butte high on a ridge to the south from the road at 0.8 miles from the bridge (20.0 miles from I-70). Park wherever looks the closest and hike south to the butte. It's a 45-minute hike. Woody's Roofs are not obvious until you are below the northeast prow of Bottleneck Peak. It ascends a thin crack system on the prow, then larger cracks and roofs above.

Route: Pitch 1: Climb a right-facing corner to a ledge, then aid up a widening, left-angling crack for a full rope length. Pitch 2: Continue up the crack to a decent ledge and fixed anchors (5.10+, A1). Pitch 3: Climb the off-width crack/chimney system for a full rope length to a stance (5.10+). Pitch 4: Climb a chimney (5.9+) to a belay. Then scramble to the summit.

Special considerations: Although it is still considered a nailing route, this route will likely be done clean soon. Two-hundred-foot ropes are helpful.

Descent: Rappel the Langdon Route, which lies 100 feet to the right of Woody's Roofs.

98 BOTTLENECK PEAK, TIPPIN' THE BOTTLE

First ascent: Mike Pennings and Doug Hall, November, 1993
Difficulty: IV, 5.11+
Time: 1 full day
Equipment: 2 sets of camming units; 1 set of TCUs; 1 set of stoppers
Approach: Bottleneck Peak is the obvious butte high on a ridge to the south from the road at 0.8 miles from the bridge (20 miles from I-70). Park wherever looks

the closest and hike south to the butte. It's a 45-minute hike. Tippin' the Bottle lies just 50 feet around the corner to the right of the Woody's Roofs route (climb 97), on the northwest side of Bottleneck Peak.

Route: Pitch 1: Climb a shallow corner past broken blocks to a small roof, the "Banana Splitter," above. Lay-back over another small roof and, after a full rope length, belay using camming units in a right-trending crack system. Pitch 2: Climb a right-angling crack, then surmount a weird slot (5.10+). Climb a widening finger crack above the slot (5.11+) that ends at a nice belay ledge. Pitch 3: Climb a bulge into an alcove, then through the roof of the alcove (5.11+). Climb a flake and blocks to easier ground and a belay. Pitch 4: Scramble to the summit (Class 4).

Special considerations: There is no fixed gear on the route. The third pitch of this route follows the third pitch of the Langdon Route, which was first climbed by Jim Langdon, June 1973.

Descent: Rappel the Langdon Route, which lies 100 feet to the right of Woody's Roofs (climb 97).

99 WINDOW BLIND PEAK, NORTH RIB

First ascent: Hal Gribble, Paul Horton, Renny Jackson, Roger Jackson, Guy Toombes, and Cindy Wilbur, February 19, 1977
Difficulty: II, 5.7
Time: 1 full day
Equipment: 1 set of camming units; 1 set of TCUs

Window Blind Peak from the north. The North Rib follows a rib above the sunlit tower in the center of the face. © Cameron M. Burns.

Approach: Window Blind Peak, the large butte lying just southeast of Assembly Hall Peak, is best approached as a hike from the road just south of Bottleneck Peak. Park anywhere along the road south of Bottleneck Peak that looks nearest to the long hike east to Window Blind Peak. The hike takes about an hour. The North Rib is obvious. It is a low-angled prow of rock between the two "windows" on the north side of the formation. The rib is best accessed by climbing an easy chimney on the west side of the base of the rib. It can also be accessed via the east side of the rib.

Route: Pitch 1: Ascend the rib, using discontinuous cracks for protection (5.7). Pitch 2: Climb a shallow "trench" (5.5). Pitch 3: Scramble up ramps leading to the right, to the summit (Class 4).

Special considerations: There are many possible variations to this route.

Descent: Rappel the route.

SOUTHERN SAN RAFAEL SWELL

100 FAMILY BUTTE MIDDLE TOWER, DAUGHTER

First ascents: James Garrett and Alan Murphy, October 29, 1990. *First free ascent:* Mike Friedrichs and Gene Roush, 1991.

Difficulty: II, 5.10+, C1 or 5.11

Time: ½ day

Family Butte, San Rafael Swell. Daughter is the third summit from the left.
© Cameron M. Burns.

Equipment: 2 sets of Friends; 1 set of TCUs

Approach: From where you parked, hike up through a short cliff band to the mesa top, then hike west about a mile to the towers.

Route: Pitch 1: Climb up into the notch between the Middle Tower of Family Butte and the tower to the left, south (5.9). Pitch 2: Climb a right-angling crack to a stance (5.11 or 5.10, C1). Pitch 3: Continue up the crack to a bolt-protected face and the summit (5.10+, C1 or 5.11).

Special considerations: Pitch 1 is loose.

Descent: Rappel off the north side of the tower.

101 TURKEY TOWER, MR. TAMBOURINE MAN

First ascent: Mike Friedrichs and James Garrett, January 1990

Difficulty: II, 5.11, C1 or 5.9, C1

Time: ½ day

Equipment: 3 sets of Friends; 1 set of TCUs

Approach: From the road, walk 0.5 mile to the tower, then around to the southwest

Climb 101, Turkey Tower, Mr. Tambourine Man. © Cameron M. Burns.

face of Turkey Tower, above a large slope. Tambourine Man follows a corner system in the middle of the southwest face.

Route: Pitch 1: Climb the corner system past a broken ledge (5.9), then up a steep section, then out under a roof to belay slings at the edge of the roof (5.11 or C1). Pitch 2: Continue up the corner system for 30 feet, until it is possible to face-climb to the right past several bolts to a notch below the summit block (5.10+). Pitch 3: Scramble over to the obvious bolt ladder and climb it to the summit (C1).

Descent: Rappel the south face of the tower.

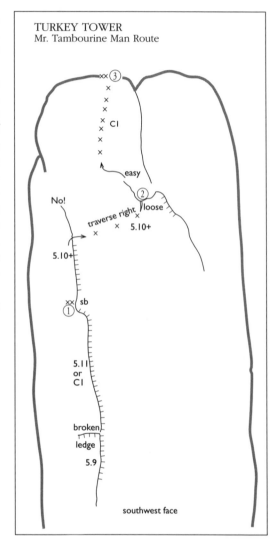

TURKEY TOWER
Mr. Tambourine Man Route

SOUTHWESTERN UTAH

ZION NATIONAL PARK

Zion Canyon is one of the grandest features in the desert Southwest. With its 2,000-foot red, orange, and yellow sandstone walls, its fantastic creeks and waterfalls, and an incredible abundance of wildlife, it's no wonder the canyon's early Mormon settlers believed they had found a place worthy of a Biblical name.

For rock climbers seeking big-wall challenges, Zion is really the only place in the United States that compares with Yosemite Valley. While not quite as big as some of El Cap's routes, Zion routes can be every bit as challenging. Soft rock, old and missing bolts, and tricky route-finding are the least of the problems you might experience on a Zion wall. As John Middendorf once said, "A thousand feet of sandstone feels like 2,000 feet of granite."

You'll notice after you've spent some time in the place that the best routes in Zion climb the lower 1,000 to 1,200 feet of the canyon's Navajo sandstone: the highly cemented red rock. The majority of these routes (Touchstone Wall, climb 111, and Space Shot, climb 121, for example) lie in the northern portion of the canyon, where the gorge necks down and the Virgin River snakes between vertical cliffs. Lower down in the canyon one generally finds longer routes that push up into the yellow Navajo sandstone. While the yellow rock can be poor at times and extremely weak after rain, there are a number of high-quality climbs that break through it to reach the canyon rim. These routes are true adventures.

Area regulations: Climbers should check at the visitor center for the current status of climbing in the park. Certain formations can be closed for nesting raptors. Zion National Park does allow the use of pitons and the placement of bolts; however, the park service asks climbers to not place fixed gear unless an existing anchor is deemed unsafe. Motorized drills are prohibited.

Special considerations: Most routes in Zion follow single crack systems, which often vary only fractions of an inch in size between pitches. The technique of leapfrogging gear (placing it, then removing gear below you) is a good one to learn and be comfortable with before you start up any Zion route. It is also not a bad idea to consider 200-foot ropes the standard in Zion.

One thing might turn you off on your first visit: Nearly ever Zion route begins with one or two jungle pitches that lead to the real route. These jungle pitches can be nasty, unpleasant pains in the neck, and cause you to get totally lost. Treat them with respect. It is extremely helpful to scope your route with binoculars before you start up it.

Also, when most climbers think of big-wall routes in Zion, they think of nailing, and in terms of A1, A2, A3, etc. The routes in this guidebook will pleasantly surprise you. In many instances, climbers who have historically put up wall routes have recorded aid sections with "A" ratings, even if these sections were done on camming units and stoppers. The current trend is to draw topos with a "C" rating. I've tried to switch from A to C on topos in this chapter wherever I knew routes had definitely been done clean. But if a topo says A1 (or whatever) and seems outdated, ignore the rating and try to do the pitch as clean as you can.

Most important of all: Descents are the crux of every Zion route. Be prepared to get yourself down under every type of condition. By comparison with the ascent routes, the descents are extremely tricky. These are big walls and should be respected as such.

Getting to Zion Canyon: Zion Canyon is a roughly 10-mile-long, north-south-oriented canyon in southwestern Utah, roughly 43 miles northeast of the city of St. George on I-15 and just north of the town of Springdale, Utah, on Hwy. 9. From Springdale, drive north on Hwy. 9 and reach the park entrance (at the south end of the canyon) just outside of town. The mileage log, below, of formations within the main canyon (Zion Canyon) and where they are located begins at the T intersection where the main Zion Canyon Road and the Mount Carmel Highway (Hwy. 9) meet, exactly 1.5 miles north of the park gate at Springdale. This list of rock formations and the routes on them is simply to help first-time visitors locate routes. It is not intended to be your parking directions. There are many small automobile pulloffs throughout Zion National Park where climbers can park for routes, and such considerations are best left up to each individual climbing party. However, it is imperative that climbers (like everyone else) park properly, in designated parking areas, with their vehicle completely off the main road. During the summer and fall months, the main canyon gets bumper-to-bumper traffic, and climbers need to do their best not to create problems for other visitors.

Mileage	Formation and/or Route
1.2	Right Twin Brother (on the right), Peyote Dreams (climb 102)
1.6	Mountain of the Sun (on the right), The Tao of Light (climb 103) and Eye Shadow (climb 104)
1.7	Court of the Patriarchs (on the left), Tricks of the Tramp (climb 105) and Sands of Time (climb 106)
2.5	Mount Moroni (on the left), Smoot-Ellison (climb 107)
3.0	Zion Lodge area/Spearhead Mountain (on the left), Iron Messiah (climb 108)
3.7	Grotto Picnic Area and West Rim Trail (to Angel's Landing), Red Arch Mountain (on the right), Wigs in Space (climb 109)
5.2	Muralla del Sol (on the right), Beyond the Pale (climb 110)
5.3	Cerebrus Gendarme (on the right), Touchstone Wall (climb 111)
5.5	The Organ (climb 112), Angel's Landing (climb 113), and The Minotaur (climbs 114 and 115) (all on the left)
5.6	Cerebrus Gendarme's back area (on the right), Magic Carpet Ride (climb 116)

5.8   Moonlight Buttress (on the left) (climbs 117 and 118) and Swoop Gimp (climb 119)

6.0   Desert Shield Buttress (on the right), Desert Shield (climb 120)

6.2   Leaning Wall (on the right), Space Shot (climb 121); Swoop Gimp (climb 119) (across the river on the large pink Moonlight Buttress)

6.6   Temple of Sinawava parking area (on the right), Monkeyfinger (climb 122)

6.7   Temple of Sinawava parking area, the Pulpit (climb 123), etc. (on the left)

Getting to Pine Creek Canyon: While most people think of Zion as having one canyon, Pine Creek Canyon meets Zion Canyon near Zion Canyon's bottom end and comes in from the east; it has numerous classic routes. The description below of formations in Pine Creek Canyon and where they are located begins at the T intersection of the main canyon road and the Zion–Mount Carmel Highway, which lies within the park exactly 1.5 miles north of the park gate at Springdale.

From this T intersection, drive east up the Mount Carmel Highway (Hwy. 9) for 0.5 mile. On the left (north) side of the road is a small pullout just before a bridge. This is the best parking spot for routes on East Temple (climbs 124–127). To reach the Tunnels Area routes, continue about 3.5 miles along the Mount Carmel Highway until the last switchback and the start of the Tunnels. Roughly 0.1 mile before the entrance of the first tunnel is a small yellow sign that says "Narrow Tunnel, Low Clearances, Sharp Curves." On the slope above this sign, about 70 feet from the road, is the small leaning tower of Ashtar Command. The standard route on the tower (North Face, climb 128) faces the road. To reach The Headache and Masterblaster, park along the north side of the road, then hike toward the first tunnel. Do not enter the tunnel, however; walk around its outside for 50 feet and The Headache (climb 129), a stunning, obvious, three-pitch hand crack, becomes obvious above the trail. Masterblaster (climb 130) lies another 170 feet to the left up the hill and on the left side of a wide gully. The route climbs to a steep, clean crack that splits a roof left of the gully.

Getting to the Lower Canyon: To reach the Three Marys, from the southern park entrance drive south through Springdale on Hwy. 9 for 0.7 mile from the park gate. On the right (west) side of the road is a road leading to the "Dixie College: Obert C. Tanner Amphitheater." Follow this road for about 0.7 mile to its end at a locked gate. Although parking is not allowed here, this is a good place to drop off your partner and gear for Gentleman's Agreement (climb 131). Parking is found back along the main road.

To reach Mount Kinesava, continue south on Hwy. 9 for several miles until you see mile marker 29. Just 0.15 mile south of mile marker 29 is a paved road leading west, up a steep hill, to the Anasazi Plateau subdivision. Drive a few hundred feet up this road, and the parking lot for the Chinle Trail is obvious on the right. Follow the Chinle Trail for about 3 miles to the base of the south face of Mount Kinesava.

ZION CANYON

102 RIGHT TWIN BROTHER, PEYOTE DREAMS

First ascent: Eric Rasmussen and Sean Plunkett, November 1995
Difficulty: VI, 5.10, A3+–A4-
Time: 3–4 days
Equipment: 8 Birdbeaks; 15 KB; 15 LA; 5 ½-inch; 5 ⅝-inch; 2 ¾-inch; 2 1-inch; 1 1¼-inch; 1 1¾-inch; 3 sets of Friends; 3 sets of TCUs; 1 #4 Camalot; stoppers; a decent selection of hooks

Approach: From the T intersection of Zion Canyon Road–Mount Carmel Highway, drive about 1.2 miles on Zion Canyon Road. Hike up to the base of the Right Twin Brother. Peyote Dreams begins near the right-hand end of the Banzai Pipeline, a strange, tubular-shaped band of rock that undercuts the wall above, and climbs a devious line of discontinuous cracks, corners, and faces up the center of the Right Twin Brother.

Route: Pitch 1: Climb several bolts through the Banzai Pipeline, then a right-angling thin crack leading to a sling belay just to the right of a right-facing corner (A2). Pitch 2: Climb the roof above (A3), then follow the obvious crack straight up to a belay. Pitch 3: Scramble up to a huge ledge and belay. Move left on the ledge 100 feet. Pitch 4: Climb a left-facing corner to bolts, then a left-trending ramp. Belay below a right-facing, arching corner. Pitch 5: Climb the arching corner, then move left out of

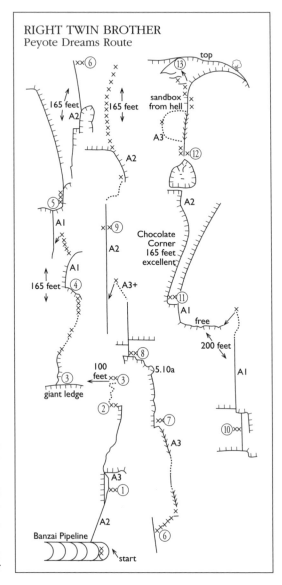

RIGHT TWIN BROTHER
Peyote Dreams Route

it and up a short bolt ladder to a pendulum leading to an A1 crack. Belay at an obvious ledge. Pitch 6: Climb past a few bolts in the enormous left-leaning corner above the belay, move around the outside of the corner via a small crack system, then climb a left-facing corner to a stance, then a crack above the stance on the left side of a small pillar (A2). Pitch 7: Move to the right on bolts, then follow a funky slot (A3) to a belay at the base of a right-facing corner. Pitch 8: Climb the corner (5.10a) to its top and a decent ledge. Pitch 9: Climb the crack above the ledge, then move up and left (A3+), pendulum left, and climb an A2 crack to a sling belay. Pitch 10: Continue up the crack, then move right, to a bolt at the base of a left-leaning arch. Climb the arch (A2), then escape out the top via a bolt ladder. Pitch 11: Move slightly left around a square roof, then climb the crack above to a pendulum left, then move along a ledge to the left. Aid up a short section (A1) to reach the base of the Chocolate Corner (200-foot lead). Pitch 12: Follow the corner to the left of the belay (not the corner to the right of the belay) to its top, then move left around a detached flake and belay atop the flake (A2). Pitch 13: Climb around the crack above (the "sandbox from hell") by moving left (A3) past a bolt, then back into the crack. Bolts and roofs lead to the top.

Special considerations: This is one of the hardest routes in this guidebook and deserving of much respect. Two-hundred-foot ropes are mandatory. Also, the above gear list is the most current, but much of the route likely goes clean, so consider that when racking.

Descent: The descent is a combination of rappelling and scrambling down the obvious slabs to the south (right) of Right Twin Brother.

103 MOUNTAIN OF THE SUN, THE TAO OF LIGHT

First ascent: John Middendorf and Paul Turecki, 1994
Difficulty: VI, 5.10, A3
Time: 3–4 days
Equipment: 3 sets of camming units and TCUs; 2 sets of stoppers; a selection of 20 thin to medium pitons

Approach: From the T intersection of Zion Canyon Road–Mount Carmel Highway, drive about 1.6 miles on Zion Canyon Road. Mountain of the Sun is on your right. The Tao of Light ascends the obvious arête on the right side of Mountain of the Sun's west face. The route starts to the right of a huge red arch on the west face.

Route: Pitch 1: Class 3 climbing leads to the base of a short chimney. Pitch 2: Climb the chimney (5.7) to a large ramp that leads right. Pitch 3: Climb the Class 3 ramp to its right-hand end. Pitch 4: Climb a long (220-foot) flake on its right side (5.10, A1) to a stance. Pitch 5: Work up and right to a huge bushy ledge (Class 3). Move along the ledge to its right-hand end, and belay atop a small pillar. Pitch 6: Climb a wide 5.8 left-facing corner to a belay at a ledge. Pitch 7: Mantle up and right, past a couple of bolts, then aid (A2+) out, right, under a roof, then back left in a right-facing corner to a large ledge. Pitch 8: Work right, on easy ground, then climb a splitter A1 crack to a small ledge. Pitch 9: Work right and climb a 5.8 chimney, then a 5.10 crack with some loose material to fixed anchors. Pitch 10: Move right and climb a left-facing corner (5.8), then the roof out left (A3) past a bolt to a belay. Pitch 11: Work left across the prow of the arête on holes, then pendulum left to a crack. Climb the crack as it widens to a belay at fixed anchors (5.10, A3). Pitch 12: Continue up the crack (A1, 5.9). Pitch 13: Move right, along the ledge, then climb a right-facing corner to a ledge behind a small pinnacle. Pitch 14: Move right, behind the pinnacle, to a tree. Pitch 15: Climb behind the pinnacle using a left-facing corner, then the left side of a pillar to the top of the pillar (A3, 5.10). Pitch 16: Move right, on the ledge, then climb the roof to the right to a belay around the corner of the arête (A3). Pitch 17: Climb the large right-facing corner above the belay to easy ground, then move right, on Class 4 ground, to a belay. Pitches 18–19: Climb straight up on Class 4 ground to the top.

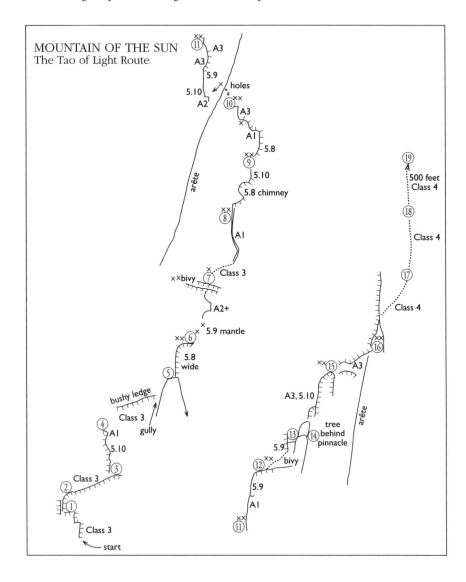

Mountain of the Sun from the southwest: climb 104, Eye Shadow; climb 103, The Tao of Light. © Cameron M. Burns.

Special considerations: There are good bivy ledges atop pitches 7 and 12. Two-hundred-foot ropes are mandatory. This is a serious and committing route.

Descent: Rappel the route, or descend the back side.

104 MOUNTAIN OF THE SUN, EYE SHADOW

First ascent: Warren Hollinger and Cameron Burns, October 1996
Difficulty: VI, 5.9, A2+
Time: 3–4 days
Equipment: 3 sets of camming units to #5 Camalot; 3 sets of TCUs or equivalent; stoppers; a selection of 20 small pitons; 10 Birdbeaks

Warren Hollinger following pitch 9, Eye Shadow, Zion National Park.
© Cameron M. Burns.

Approach: From the T intersection of Zion Canyon Road–Mount Carmel Highway, drive about 1.6 miles on Zion Canyon Road. Mountain of the Sun is on the right. Eye Shadow starts up a long, right-angling chimney system on the right side of the lower wall on the west face.

Route: Pitches 1–2: Scramble up Class 4 ground to reach the base of the huge chimney. Pitches 3–4: Climb the chimney to its top (5.9, C1). Pitch 5: Move left, around the corner on a ledge, and belay at anchors. Pitch 6: Climb the splitter above the ledge (A1) to Mascara Ledge. Pitches 7–9: Scramble up and left, skirting the left edge of a huge bowl below the big red arch. Belay on huge ledges at a Big Tree overlooking the bowl (Class 4–lower Class 5). Pitch 10: From the Big Tree work out right, in thin cracks, to a belay at fixed anchors. Pitch 11: Pendulum right and continue up to the base of the "Eye." Pitch 12: Climb the crack up the center of the Eye (A1), turn the roof (A2+), then belay at a ledge. Pitch 13: Move right, up a ramp (easy Class 5) and the corner above, then move right slightly and head for a tree below another roof. Nail the roof above (A1), then move up and right, to a bolt. Continue right, to another seam (5.9), which leads to a stance and anchors. Pitch 14: Move up and left past a bolt to the base of a prominent chimney (5.9 R). Climb the chimney. Pitch 15: Climb loose Class 4 ground up and left to the base of a huge, right-facing corner. Pitch 16: Climb the corner to the top (C1). Pitch 17: Scramble to the summit.

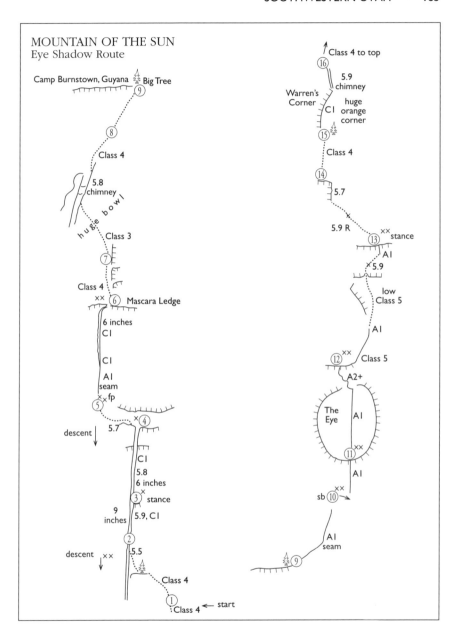

MOUNTAIN OF THE SUN
Eye Shadow Route

Special considerations: Two-hundred-foot ropes are mandatory. Decent bivy ledges are located atop pitch 9 at the Big Tree ("Camp Burnstown, Guyana"). Pitch 13 requires some tricky routefinding.

Descent: Rappel the route to the Big Tree (atop pitch 9), then make several rappels straight down to the top of pitch 7. Rappel pitches 7 and 6, then rappel straight down to the ground.

105 ISAAC, TRICKS OF THE TRAMP

First ascent: John Middendorf, Brad Quinn, and Bill Hatcher, April 1993 (Calvin Hebert worked on the lower pitches)

Difficulty: VI, 5.11+, A2

Time: 2–3 days

Equipment: 3 sets of camming units to #5 Camalot; 3 sets of TCUs; stoppers; a small selection of thin pitons

Approach: From the T intersection of Zion Canyon Road–Mount Carmel Highway, drive about 1.7 miles on Zion Canyon Road to a parking spot along the road. Hike about an hour into the Court of the Patriarchs and head for Isaac, the central of the three patriarchs. From below Isaac, head for the "toe" of the most prominent central buttress on the formation. Tricks of the Tramp starts in a clean, 4-inch-wide crack, 50 feet to the right of a huge chimney system on the outside of the buttress.

Route: Pitch 1: Climb a 5.10 off-width past a couple of bolts to a stance on the left. Pitch 2: Continue straight up past a couple more bolts to a fixed belay (5.9). Pitches 3–4: Work to the left into the huge chimney system and climb it for two pitches (5.8, 5.7). Pitch 5: Scramble up and left to the base of The Calvinator, a long, wide crack. Pitch 6: Climb The Calvinator (5.10) to a ledge and fixed anchors. Pitches 7–9: Climb three pitches of mostly Class 4 ground (up to 5.7) to gain a large ledge in front of a short pillar. Pitches 10–11: Move right, past a ledge, and climb the right side of the pillar (5.10+ off-width) to its top and a belay ledge. Pitch 12: Climb up and right, following a 5.10+ hand crack to a double pendulum right and a bolted belay at the end of the swings. Pitch 13: Climb a right-facing corner (5.9), then an A2 crack to a stance. Pitch 14: Climb the obvious 5.10

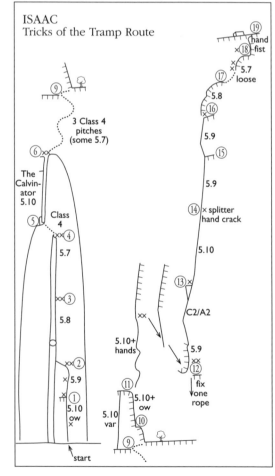

splitter hand crack above the belay. Pitches 15–16: Continue up the splitter to belay at stances on the right (5.9, 5.9). Pitch 17: Move left around the top of an arching flake (5.8). Pitch 18: Move up and right, over loose 5.7 ground, past several bolts to belay on a ledge with a bolt. Pitch 19: Step right and climb the hand/fist crack to the top.

Special considerations: All but 60 feet of the route has been done free. There is much off-width climbing.

Descent: Continue to the summit of Isaac, then scramble down slabs to the northeast. Several rappels may be necessary to gain the drainage between Isaac and Jacob (the Patriarch to the east of Isaac). Hike down the drainage into a hanging valley, then make several more rappels to reach the ground.

Isaac: climb 106, Sands of Time; climb 105, Tricks of the Tramp.
© Cameron M. Burns.

106 ISAAC, SANDS OF TIME

First ascent: Paul Gagner and Rick Lovelace, 1994
Difficulty: VI, 5.10, A3+
Time: 3–4 days
Equipment: 3 sets of camming units to #5 Camalot; 3 sets of TCUs;
stoppers; a small selection of thin pitons; 15 Birdbeaks

Approach: From the T intersection of Zion Canyon Road–Mount Carmel
Highway, drive about 1.7 miles on Zion Canyon Road to a parking spot along the
road. Hike about an hour into the Court of the Patriarchs and head for Isaac, the
central of the three patriarchs. The route starts in a 5.9 off-width around the corner
from (to the left of) Tricks of the Tramp (climb 105).

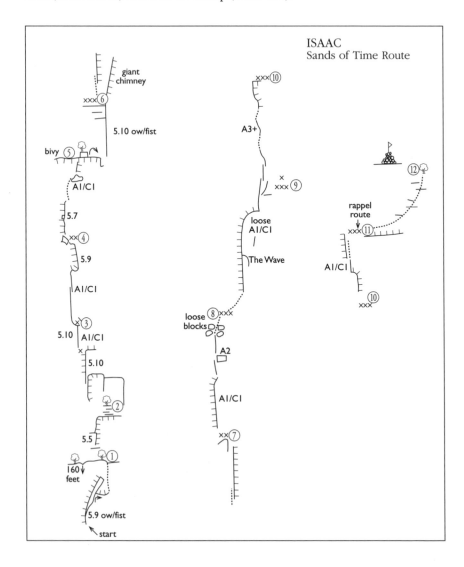

Route: Pitch 1: Climb a right-angling off-width/fist crack, undercling to the right under a roof, then climb to a large ledge (5.9). Pitch 2: Climb an easy left-facing corner to a large ledge (5.5). Pitch 3: Work up and left to a wide crack on the left side of a block, then climb it into a right-facing corner (5.10). Work left out the corner of the roof past a bolt and up an A1 crack to a belay. Pitch 4: Move left and climb an A1 crack to an undercling right (5.9) and up to a belay at fixed anchors. Pitch 5: Climb a right-facing corner (5.7), then move up and right, past a block to a ledge. Pitch 6: Move right, on the ledge, down-climb a few feet, then climb a splitter off-width/fist crack to a fixed belay (5.10). Pitch 7: Climb a left-facing corner left of a huge chimney to a point with a fixed belay. Pitch 8: A right-facing A1 corner leads to some stacked loose blocks (A2), then a fixed belay. Pitch 9: Work right, into the base of The Wave, a

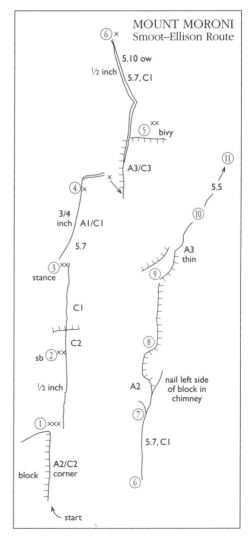

MOUNT MORONI
Smoot–Ellison Route

huge, right-leaning arch. Climb The Wave (A1/C1) to a bolted belay above and right of the top of the arch. Pitch 10: Continue up discontinuous cracks (A3+ beaks) to a left-facing corner with a decent stance at the top of the corner and fixed anchors. Pitch 11: Climb a left-facing corner through a roof, then a right-facing corner to a fixed anchor (A1/C1). Pitch 12: Scramble up and right, on easy ground to the top of the buttress. (The route does not go to the top of the peak. See photo.)

Special considerations: There is some loose rock. There is a decent bivy ledge at the top of pitch 5, but bring a long (50-foot) piece of webbing to tie off a block there (no fixed anchors).

Descent: Rappel the route.

107 MOUNT MORONI, SMOOT-ELLISON

First ascent: Brian Smoot and Les Ellison, April 1984 (Jonathon and Brian Smoot climbed half the route in 1982)
Difficulty: IV, 5.10, A3
Time: 1–2 days

Climb 107, Mount Moroni, Smoot-Ellison. © Cameron M. Burns.

Equipment: 3 sets of camming units; 3 sets of TCUs or equivalent, stoppers; a selection of thin pitons; hooks

Approach: From the T intersection of Zion Canyon Road–Mount Carmel Highway, drive about 2.5 miles on Zion Canyon Road. Mount Moroni is on the left. The route begins in the center of the east face's largest wall, and starts on the right side of a square block with a slightly pointed top right corner sitting at the base of the face.

Route: Pitch 1: Climb the right side of the block to a belay (A2). Pitches 2–3: Climb the ½-inch crack straight up for two pitches (C2, C1) to a sling belay. Pitch 4: Move right, on a 5.7 ramp, then climb a ¾-inch crack to a fixed belay. Pitch 5: Move up and right, around a roof, then pendulum right, into a crack in a right-facing corner. Continue up the crack to a spacious ledge (bivy). Pitch 6: Follow the left-trending crack (5.7, C1) to a belay in an off-width pod. Pitch 7: Continue up the crack above (5.7, C1) to the base of a chimney. Pitch 8: Climb the left side of the block in the chimney (A2), then move left out a left-facing corner and belay at a ledge. Pitch 9: Continue up the left-facing corner to a stance below a roof. Pitch 10: Move right, up a ramp (A3) to a belay. Pitch 11: Easy free-climbing leads to the top.

Special considerations: If it hasn't already, this route will likely go clean.

Descent: Rappel off the west side of the summit, then scramble north to gain the Lady Mountain Trail. Follow it back to the road.

108 SPEARHEAD MOUNTAIN, IRON MESSIAH

First ascents: Ron Olevsky, 1988. *First free ascent:* Darren Cope and Jeff Rickerl, 1989.

Difficulty: III–IV, 5.10

Time: 1 full day

Equipment: 2 sets of camming units; 1 set of TCUs; 1 set of stoppers

Climb 108, Spearhead Mountain, Iron Messiah. © Cameron M. Burns.

Approach: From the T intersection of Zion Canyon Road–Mount Carmel Highway, drive about 3 miles on Zion Canyon Road. Spearhead Mountain is on the left. Get to the route by eyeballing the huge corner the route follows, then scramble up a left-to-right ramp system (Class 4) that leads to the base of a brown wall with bolts.

Route: Pitch 1: Climb a bolted face just to the right of the base of the corner (5.10a) to a big ledge. Pitch 2: Move left slightly and climb a crack to the top of a triangular point with a bolt (5.7). Pitches 3–7: Work right, into the huge corner, then climb it for five pitches—(5.10), (5.9), (5.9), (5.9), (5.9+)—until the seventh pitch, which moves right, at the top of the corner onto a large ledge. Pitch 8: Climb a 5.10 crack to the top of a pointed pillar. Pitch 9: Easy 5.4 ground leads to the top.

Special considerations: There is a bolted three-pitch variation left of pitch 2 that is not recommended. Climbers seem to either love or hate this route for some reason.

Descent: Rappel the route.

109 RED ARCH MOUNTAIN, WIGS IN SPACE

First ascent: Cameron "Wigfoot" Burns, James "Bad Hair" Garrett, and Chris "Wiggy Stardust" Eng, March 1999. (The first four pitches were climbed by Cam Burns, Pete Doorish, and Fred Beckey, April 1998.) *First free ascent:* Jeff Hollenbaugh and Cameron Tague, June 1999.

Difficulty: IV, 5.9, A1 or IV, 5.11

Time: 1–2 days

Equipment: 3 sets of camming units to #5 Camalot; 2 sets of TCUs; 2 sets of stoppers; 1 Birdbeak; 1 small hook; 2 KB; 2 LA; 200-foot ropes helpful

Approach: From the T intersection of Zion Canyon Road–Mount Carmel Highway, drive 3.7 miles on Zion Canyon Road upcanyon. Red Arch Mountain is on the right. Wigs in Space climbs an obvious set of flakes and corners on the flat-faced southwest buttress of Red Arch Mountain. The route starts at the buttress's lowest point on the hillside.

Route: Pitch 1: Climb a wide, easy chimney (5.6) to a left-facing corner. Climb the corner (C1) to the top. (The Hollenbaugh-Tague free version climbs a fingercrack on the face, a few feet left of the corner, at 5.10-). Pitch 2: Scramble up and left to a huge bushy ledge (Class 4). Pitch 3: Scramble up a slab (5.7) to a right-angling ramp and climb the ramp to a two-bolt belay at the base of the "Afro Cracks" (5.7). Pitch 4: Climb the thin Afro Cracks above the ledge (5.11 or C1) around a left-arching roof system(5.10 or C1), then move right, onto a spacious belay (5.6). Pitch 5: Climb the right side of a detached block (5.9 or 5.8, A1), then move left past a wide chimney to several bolts that lead to a wide crack behind a flake. Climb the wide crack to the "Hair Club for Men Ledge." (The Hollenbaugh-Tague free version climbs the chimney at 5.8.) Pitch 6: Climb the awkward, left-arching, "Bad Hair Bombay Slot" above the ledge (5.10 or 5.9, C1), then exit right, past two bolts to a bolted belay stance. Pitch 7: Climb the stunning corner above the belay ("The Bouffant Blast") around the arching roof (5.7, C1) to the "Wigs Out!" hanging belay. (The Hollenbaugh-Tague free version climbs halfway up the corner before moving out

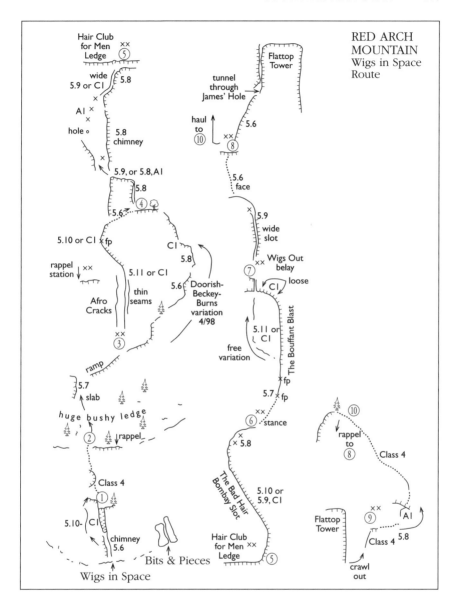

left onto the face to join a splitter hand crack (5.10) that leads to the belay.) Pitch 8: Climb the wide, left-arching slot above the belay (5.9) past a bolt, and exit the slot at its highest point. Face-climb (5.6) to a perfect triangular ledge. Pitch 9: Climb the ramp leading right, to the base of "Flattop Tower" (5.6), then worm through James' Hole behind the tower to a belay at two bolts. Pitch 10: Move right for 30 feet, nail (A1) a short bulge, then climb Class 4 rock to the top of the buttress.

Special considerations: The first ascent party placed about 6 pitons, because they had no stoppers on the first five pitches. The first three pitches can be broken

Cam Burns on the "Afro Cracks," Wigs In Space, Red Arch Mountain, Zion National Park. Photo: James Garrett/Burns collection.

up in many different ways, depending on the party's preference. Finally, it is best to travel light on the last two pitches, as James' Hole is extremely tight. A single fixed rope reaches easily from the top of pitch 10 straight down to the top of pitch 8. A 50-foot piece of webbing is recommended to replace the summit anchor. As this book was going to press, the route was free-climbed by Jeff Hollenbaugh and Cameron Tague at 5.11.

Descent: Rappel the route.

110 MURALLA DEL SOL, BEYOND THE PALE

First ascent: Mike Baker and Chris Ducker, October 1996 (Kendall Taylor, Ty Callahan, and Leslie Henderson worked on lower pitches)
Difficulty: VI, 5.11a, A3
Time: 3 days
Equipment: 2 sets of stoppers; 2 sets of TCUs; 2 sets of Camalots (#0.5–#5); Tri Cams to #2; 3 Birdbeaks; 4 knifeblades; 2 LA; angles from ½ inch to 1 inch; several small hooks

Approach: From the T intersection of Zion Canyon Road–Mount Carmel Highway, drive 5.2 miles on Zion Canyon Road. Muralla del Sol is on the right.

Route: Pitch 1: Climb a bolt-protected slab (5.11a) for 145 feet to a three-bolt belay. Pitch 2: Climb past one bolt (5.9+), then climb an easy slab to belay at a tree (155 feet). Pitch 3: Climb Class 3 ground up and left to the base of a left-facing

Left: *Climb 109, Red Arch Mountain, Wigs in Space.* © Cameron M. Burns.

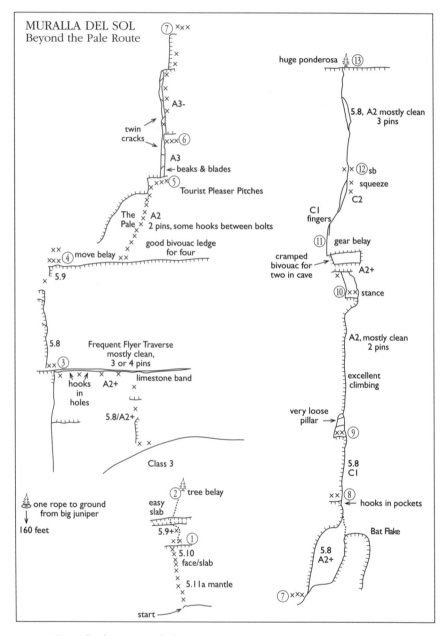

MURALLA DEL SOL
Beyond the Pale Route

(7) ×××

×
×
×

× A3-
×
×

twin
cracks ××× (6)

A3

←beaks & blades

××× (5)

Tourist Pleaser Pitches

The × A2
Pale × 2 pins, some hooks between bolts
×

good bivouac ledge
for four

×× (4) move belay ××

5.9

huge ponderosa (13)

5.8, A2 mostly clean
3 pins

×× (12) sb
× squeeze
× C2

C1
fingers

(11) gear belay

cramped
bivouac for
two in cave

A2+

(10) ×× stance

A2, mostly clean
2 pins

excellent
climbing

very loose
pillar →

×× (9)

5.8
C1

5.8
Frequent Flyer Traverse
mostly clean,
3 or 4 pins
×× (3)
× × × × limestone band
hooks A2+ ×
in
holes ×
5.8/A2+
× ×

Class 3

(2) tree belay
easy
slab

one rope to ground
from big juniper

160 feet

5.9+×

×× (1)

× 5.10

× face/slab
×
× 5.11a mantle
×
×

start

×× (8)
← hooks in pockets

Bat Flake

5.8
A2+

(7) ×××

corner. Face-climb past two bolts (5.8) to gain the corner proper. At the top of the corner, aid straight up, passing several drilled anchors with several pin placements. Gain a horizontal limestone band. Aid (A2+) left along the limestone band on beaks, hooks, and fixed gear to a belay at the base of a right-facing corner. Pitch 4: Climb the right-facing corner (5.8) past a bolt, then climb a left-facing corner (5.9) to a three-bolt rappel station. Continue 15 feet past this anchor to a two-bolt anchor in

Climb 110, Muralla del Sol, Beyond the Pale. © Cameron M. Burns.

better rock to belay. At this point, it is a good idea to move the belay right, along an obvious ledge to a two-bolt anchor. (The ledge also makes a good bivouac ledge.) Pitch 5: Aid a bolt ladder (A2) with some hooks in between bolts to a three-bolt hanging belay. Pitch 6: Aid out the 6-foot roof above the belay, then nail the beak-and-blade crack above, passing a bolt, to clean aid above, before reaching a three-bolt hanging belay. Pitch 7: Move left, then aid (clean and nailing) up the twin cracks above to a three-bolt anchor at a stance. Pitch 8: Move right (5.8) to the left edge of an obvious flake (Bat Flake). At the top of the flake, step back left and gain the right-facing corner above. Aid the corner (some hooking) to a two-bolt belay on a comfortable ledge. Pitch 9: Continue up the corner (5.8, C1) to a two-bolt drilled anchor on a ledge. Pitch 10: Aid up behind a 20-foot pillar (very loose), pass a bolt, then continue up the clean corner above. The pitch finishes with a small roof, lead-ing to a two-bolt belay stance. Pitch 11: Climb up to a bolt below an overhang, and turn the overhang to reach a cave with a sloping bottom (no fixed anchors in the cave; uncomfortable bivy). Continue up above the cave to a natural gear belay. Pitch 12: Climb a gorgeous finger-sized crack (C1) to a squeeze chimney protected by two bolts, then gain a two-bolt hanging belay. Pitch 13: Continue up the crack with several piton placements, but mostly clean, to a 5.8 chimney. Climb the chimney, then continue mixed free and aid to a huge ponderosa tree.

Special considerations: This is a serious and demanding route that requires much big-wall experience. As with all Zion routes, the descent is the crux.

Descent: Standard descent is to scramble up and to the right from the top of the route for about 250 feet, then make one rappel off a tree and down-scramble to a single-bolt rappel (40 feet) to gain the top of a huge bench that makes up the southeastern portion of the Muralla del Sol. At this point, it is necessary to locate a tree at the edge of the main canyon, then rappel into the main canyon and make five double-rope rappels to the ground.

111 CEREBRUS GENDARME, TOUCHSTONE WALL

First ascent: Ron Olevsky, 1977

Difficulty: IV, 5.9, C2

Time: 1 full day

Equipment: 2 sets of camming units to #4; 2 sets of wired stoppers with extra medium stoppers and several RP nuts

Approach: From the T intersection of Zion Canyon Road–Mount Carmel Highway, drive 5.3 miles on Zion Canyon Road. Cerebrus Gendarme is on the right.

Route: Pitch 1: Climb a bolt ladder to a thin crack (C1) to a belay below a roof. Pitch 2: Climb over the roof (C2) and continue up the crack to a fixed anchor. Pitches 3–7: Continue up the ever-widening

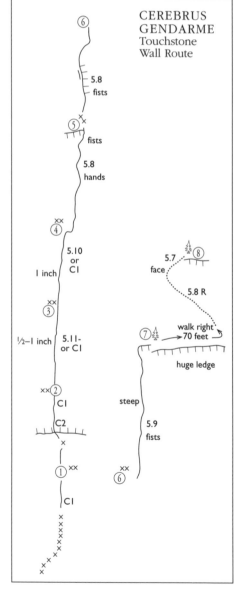

CEREBRUS GENDARME
Touchstone
Wall Route

Climb 111, Cerebrus Gendarme, Touchstone Wall. © Cameron M. Burns.

crack, using fixed anchors at belays. As the route gets higher, the free-climbing gets easier, until the seventh lead, which goes over and up an awkward 5.9 corner/roof. At the top of the seventh lead, a large ledge is reached. Pitch 8: Go back and to the left, up a steep wall behind a large pine tree. Protection and rope drag are difficult.

Special considerations: Above pitch 2, the route has been climbed all free, at 5.11-. Also, try to skip the first set of anchors on the left, three-quarters of the way up pitch 3.

Descent: From the top of the route, follow the summit ridge north (away from the route) until an obvious notch allows a descent to the right. The descent is a mixture of down-scrambling and rappelling.

112 THE ORGAN, ORGANASM

First ascent: Ron Olevsky and Mike Strassman, August 1983
Difficulty: II, 5.8, C1
Time: ½ day
Equipment: 3 sets of Friends; 1 set of TCUs; stoppers

Climb 112, The Organ, Organasm. © Cameron M. Burns.

Approach: From the T intersection of Zion Canyon Road–Mount Carmel Highway drive about 5.3–5.5 miles on Zion Canyon Road, and park where you would park for Cerebrus Gendarme or Angel's Landing. The Organ is the low butte in the crook of the river east of Angel's Landing and across the river from the Touchstone Wall (climb 111). Walk across the river to reach it. Organasm climbs a clean crack system in the northeast buttress of The Organ, in a band of very orange rock.

Route: Pitch 1: Climb the obvious corner below the chains to a sling belay (5.8, C1). Pitch 2: Climb the stunning big roof above (C1) to chains. Pitches 3–4: Continue up the crack to the top of the formation (5.7, C2).

Special considerations: The big roof reportedly goes free at 5.11+.

Descent: Many parties rappel off (with double ropes) after the first two pitches from chains atop pitch 2. If you go to the top, the descent is a combination of scrambling and rappelling to the right (northwest) of the route.

113 ANGEL'S LANDING, PRODIGAL SON

First ascent: Ron Olevsky, September 1981

Difficulty: IV, 5.8, C1

Time: 1 full day

Equipment: 1 set of camming units; several sets of wired stoppers with many medium stoppers

Approach: From the T intersection of Zion Canyon Road–Mount Carmel Highway, drive about 5.5 miles on Zion Canyon Road. Angel's Landing is on the left. The best approach is to wade the river; however, it is often running too deep to cross. If so, head downcanyon to the Zion Lodge area at 3 miles, park, and cross the river using the Angel's Landing Trail bridge. Once across this bridge, hike to the first switchback. A small, very rough trail leads down and to the right, into the underbrush. Follow this trail along the river's edge

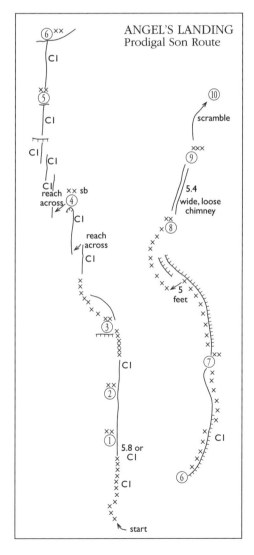

ANGEL'S LANDING
Prodigal Son Route

Above: *Climb 113, Angel's Landing, Prodigal Son.* © Cameron M. Burns. Left: *Andrew Nichols on pitch 6, Prodigal Son.* © Cameron M. Burns.

for roughly 2.5 miles to the base of the northeast face of Angel's Landing.

Route: Pitch 1: Climb a bolt ladder to a thin crack (C1). Follow this to a stance. Pitch 2: Continue up the crack (5.8 or C1). Climb a few free moves to a bolt ladder to a stance. Pitch 3: Follow bolts and thin cracks up to a ledge (C1). Pitch 4: Move left across the ledge, then continue up and left past several small dihedrals (C1) to a sling belay. Pitch 5: Continue up, following a series of thin cracks (C1). Pitch 6: Continue up the crack that gives way to a bolt ladder above the belay to a stance (C1). Pitch 7: Climb the crack above the belay to reach a good ledge (C1). Pitch 8: Climb up the large, left-facing dihedral above and right of the belay (C1). Move back left under the summit overhangs, and turn them on their left end. Belay at a ledge with fixed anchors. Pitch 9: Scramble up and right (5.4), through a chimney, and belay in a loose, sandy gully. Pitch 10: Scramble up to the trail.

Special considerations: Some parties do the route in 2 days. Rope drag can be bad on pitch 8. The exit gully above the eighth lead is really loose.

Descent: From the top of the route, hike north to join the Angel's Landing Trail. Follow this paved trail down the southwestern side of Angel's Landing to the Zion Lodge area.

114 THE MINOTAUR, THE MEGAMAHEDRAL

First ascent: "Jersey" Dave Littman and Eric Draper, June 1998 (the first few pitches had been climbed previously by Brad Quinn and Mark Austin)

Difficulty: III, 5.9+, C1

Time: 1 full day

Equipment: 3 sets of Camalots to #3; 2 #4 Camalots; 1 #5 Camalot; 1 set of stoppers

Approach: From the T intersection of Zion Canyon Road–Mount Carmel Highway, drive about 5.5 miles on Zion Canyon Road. The Minotaur is the rectangular tower with a slightly pointed top below the low point in the wall to the right of Angel's Landing. After crossing the river toward Angel's Landing, head west and The Minotaur is obvious. If the river is too high to cross, see the approach for Angel's Landing (climb 113).

Route: The route is simple.

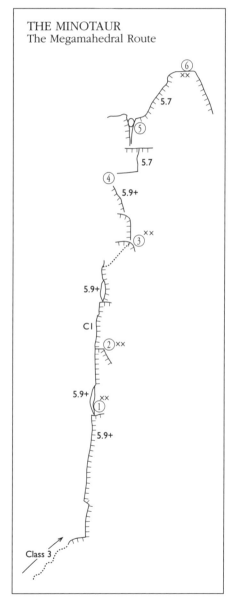

THE MINOTAUR
The Megamahedral Route

Climb the major crack/corner system on the left side of The Minotaur (when viewed from the road) to its top, six pitches.

Special considerations: Two-hundred-foot ropes are mandatory. This route will go free easily.

Descent: Rappel the route.

115 THE MINOTAUR, SUBURBAN BLONDES

First ascent: Ron Olevsky and Scott Fischer, 1979

Difficulty: IV, 5.9, A2+

Time: 1–2 days

Equipment: 2 sets of camming units to #5 Camalots; 2 sets of TCUs; stoppers

Approach: From the T intersection of Zion Canyon Road–Mount Carmel Highway, drive about 5.5 miles on Zion Canyon Road. The Minotaur is the rectangular tower with a slightly pointed top below the low point in the wall to the right of Angel's Landing. After crossing the river toward Angel's Landing, head west and The Minotaur is obvious. If the river is too high to cross, see the approach for Angel's Landing (climb 113). Suburban Blondes climbs the most obvious crack system visible from below the "front" (east face) of The Minotaur. It starts up a chimney on the right side of the enormous block sitting against the east side ("front") of the main tower.

Route: Pitch 1: Climb a 5.8 chimney to a sling belay. Pitch 2: Climb out around a scary 5-inch roof (C2), then climb a 5.9 crack to a ledge. Pitch 3: Continue up the crack/corner system to the top of the buttress (bivy ledge). Pitch 4: Pendulum right, to the base of the next wide crack system, then climb it (mixed free and clean aid) to a belay. Pitch 5: Continue up a crack just left of the prominent left-facing corner to a belay (5.9). Pitch 6: Continue straight up to the crest of the tower, then climb unprotected 5.8 to the summit.

Special considerations: This route has much wide crack and chimney climbing.

Descent: Rappel The Megamahedral with 200-foot ropes. There is reportedly also a rappel descent down the back side of the tower. The first ascent party set up a tyrolean traverse to the wall above.

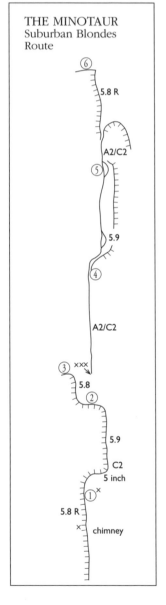

THE MINOTAUR
Suburban Blondes
Route

The Minotaur: climb 114, The Megamahedral, and climb 115, Suburban Blondes.
© Cameron M. Burns.

116 CEREBRUS GENDARME (BACK), MAGIC CARPET RIDE

First ascent: Unknown
Difficulty: IV, 5.9, A3
Time: 1–2 days
Equipment: 3 sets of camming units; 3 sets of TCUs or equivalent; stoppers; a selection of thin pitons; hooks

Approach: From the T intersection of Zion Canyon Road–Mount Carmel Highway, drive about 5.6 miles on Zion Canyon Road. The back of Cerebrus Gendarme is on the right. Scramble up a Class 5 jungle pitch to a prominent ledge. Magic Carpet Ride climbs a thin crack system on the left side (right of a huge dihedral) on the blank wall above.

Route: Pitch 1: Climb a thin crack out a roof (A3), then the crack above to a sling belay. Pitch 2: Continue up the crack to a belay below the obvious roof (A2/C2). Pitch 3: Climb a right-facing corner, then to the right, out the roof to a belay.

Climb 116, Cerebrus Gendarme (Back), Magic Carpet Ride. © Cameron M. Burns

Pitch 4: Continue up the crack to the "Zorro Crack" (a jog to the right, then back left), then a 5.7 ramp above, to a 5.9 off-width and a belay. (A2, 5.9). Pitch 5: Move left around an arch (5.8+), then back right, to a belay next to a leaning pillar. Pitch 6: Climb the slot above, then work left to a belay (5.6). Pitch 7: Scramble to the top.

Special considerations: This route will likely go clean, if it hasn't already.

Descent: Rappel the route.

117 MOONLIGHT BUTTRESS, LUNAR ECSTASY

First ascents: Linus Platt and Brad Quinn, April 1992. *First clean ascent:* Jeff Hollenbaugh and Dave Penney, spring 1996.

Difficulty: V, 5.9, C2+

Time: 2 days

Equipment: 3 sets of camming units; 3 sets of TCUs; 3 sets of RPs; 3 sets of stoppers

Approach: From the T intersection of Zion Canyon Road–Mount Carmel Highway, drive about 5.8 miles on Zion Canyon Road. Moonlight Buttress is on the left. "Lunar X," as this route is known, climbs the left side of the Moonlight Buttress formation, following the first two pitches of the Moonlight Buttress Route (climb 118).

Route: Pitch 1: Scramble up and right, through broken ledges until the climbing requires a rope. Continue up and right, to a decent ledge with a bush and fixed anchors (5.9). Pitch 2: Move up the ledge to the right, then climb a 5.10a crack around a bulge up to a ledge with fixed anchors. Pitch 3: Move up a short, right-facing corner to a decent ledge and fixed anchors (5.7, C1). Pitch 4: Continue up the crack system above to a belay (5.9). Pitch 5: Move right, then climb an overhanging left-trending crack/corner system until it turns back to the right, becoming a ramp. The ramp leads to a bolt ladder,

CEREBRUS GENDARME (BACK)
Magic Carpet Ride Route

⑦ Class 4 to top

⑥

5.6

⑤ leaning pillar

5.8+

④ ×
5.9 ow

A1/C1

Zorro Crack

5.7 ramp

A2/C2

③

A2/C2

② ×

A2/C2

① sb ×
××
A3/C3

A3/C2

huge ledge

then a decent belay ledge (5.9, C2). Pitch 6: Move up and left on a bolt ladder (C1) to join the Lunar X crack. Climb it (C2+) to a sling belay. Pitches 7–9: Continue up the crack—C1–C2+—using fixed anchors for belays. Pitch 10: Work up and right, gaining a ledge below a huge boulder (5.8, C3). Pitch 11: Climb the left side of the boulder, then a C2+ crack above to reach the top.

Special considerations: There is a variation to the start that climbs a loose 5.10 corner to the left of the start of the Moonlight Buttress Route.

Descent: From the top of the route, hike west to join the Angel's Landing Trail. Follow this paved trail down the southwestern side of Angel's Landing to the Zion Lodge area.

118 MOONLIGHT BUTTRESS, MOONLIGHT BUTTRESS ROUTE

First ascents: Jeff Lowe and Mike Weis, October 1971. *First free ascent:* Johnny Woodward and Peter Croft, April 1992.
Difficulty: IV, 5.9, C1 or 5.12d
Time: 1–2 days
Equipment: 3 sets of stoppers with extra medium stoppers; 5 sets of TCUs; 4–5 #0.5 Camalots; 3 #0.75 Camalots; 3 #1 Camalots; 3 #2 Camalots; 2 #3 Camalots

Approach: From the T intersection of Zion Canyon Road–Mount Carmel Highway, drive about 5.8 miles on Zion Canyon Road. Moonlight Buttress is on the left. Locate the Moonlight Buttress, then look down to the left of it for a bolt ladder. The route begins up two "jungle" pitches, about 150 feet left of the buttress itself, that lead to the bolt ladder.

Route: Pitch 1: Scramble up and right, through broken ledges, until the climbing requires a rope. Continue up and right, to a decent ledge with a bush and fixed anchors (5.9). Pitch 2: Move up the ledge to the right, then climb a 5.10 crack

MOONLIGHT BUTTRESS

11 10 5.7
10 9
C3
5.12a or C1
9 8
C2
5.12a or C1
8 5.6
7 5.12a or C1
C2+
7 5.12b or C1
6
C1/2
6
C2+
Lunar Ecstasy Route
5 5.12d or C1
5 4
5.9, C2
4 5.11d or C1
5.9
3
3 5.10d
C1
5.7, C1 2 2a
5.11c
Moonlight Buttress Route
1 5.10a
5.9

Moonlight Buttress area: climb 117, Lunar Ecstasy; climb 118, Moonlight Buttress route; climb 119, Upper Canyon, Swoop Gimp. © Cameron M. Burns.

around a bulge up to a ledge with fixed anchors. Pitch 3: Climb up and right, on a bolt ladder (C1) to a fixed belay. Pitch 4: Begin up the buttress proper by climbing a thin crack (5.11d or C1) to a sling belay. Pitch 5: Continue straight up to a belay beside a roof (5.12d or C1). Pitch 6: Move out the roof, then continue to a sling belay (5.12a or C1). Pitches 7–9: Continue straight up the thin crack system with belays at fixed anchors (5.12b or C1), (5.12a or C1), (5.12a or C1). Pitch 10: A 5.7 slab leads to the top.

Special considerations: This route has a lot of traffic. Pitch 3 of the regular route can be done via a free, two-pitch variation that leads out to the right from the belay atop pitch 2 via 5.11c face-climbing, then up a right-facing corner that leads to a roof (5.10d).

Descent: From the top of the route, hike west to join the Angel's Landing Trail. Follow this paved trail down the southwestern side of Angel's Landing to the Zion Lodge area.

119 UPPER CANYON, SWOOP GIMP

First ascent: Alan Humphrey and Barry Ward, 1992
Difficulty: IV, 5.9, A2+
Time: 1–2 days
Equipment: 2 LA; 2 sets of stoppers; 2 sets of HB offsets; 2 sets of TCUs; 2 sets of Camalots to #4; Leepers; hooks
Approach: From the T intersection of Zion Canyon Road–Mount Carmel Highway, drive about 5.8 miles on Zion Canyon Road. Moonlight Buttress is on the left. Swoop Gimp lies about 2,000 feet right of Moonlight Buttress and begins up a low-angled, left-to-right ramp that leads into a concave, pink-colored wall. Higher up, this wall becomes a pillar separated by two dihedrals.

Route: Pitch 1: Climb the right-angling ramp that leads to a splitter in a steep red wall

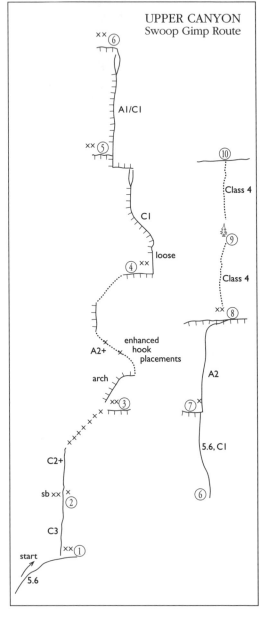

UPPER CANYON
Swoop Gimp Route

Climb 119, Upper Canyon, Swoop Gimp. © Cameron M. Burns.

(5.6). Pitch 2: Climb the splitter (C3) to a sling belay. Pitch 3: Continue up the splitter (C2+) to a bolt ladder leading to the right to a ledge. Pitch 4: Climb the arch above the ledge and out its roof, then hook past several bolts to a right-facing corner (A2+). Pitch 5: Climb some loose material, then the C1 curving crack above. Move left under a roof, then up and left to a ledge and the belay (C1). Pitch 6: Climb an A1 crack past a pod to the next ledge. Pitch 7: Continue straight up (5.6, C1). Pitch 8: Climb an A2 crack above the belay to a decent ledge (A2). Pitches 9–10: Climb Class 4 ground to the canyon rim.

Special considerations: A few months before this book went to press, the route had been done almost entirely clean. By the time you read this, it'll likely have been done entirely clean. Hauling on the upper part of this route is tough.

Descent: From the top of the route, hike southwest to join the Angel's Landing Trail. Follow this paved trail down the southwestern side of Angel's Landing to the Zion Lodge area.

120 DESERT SHIELD BUTTRESS, DESERT SHIELD

First ascents:
Unknown (first six pitches, Eric Rasmussen and Chris Sircello, 1992). *First clean ascent:* Kevin Lawlor and Mark Bennett, November 1996.

Difficulty: V, 5.11, C3

Time: 1–2 days

Equipment: 3 sets of

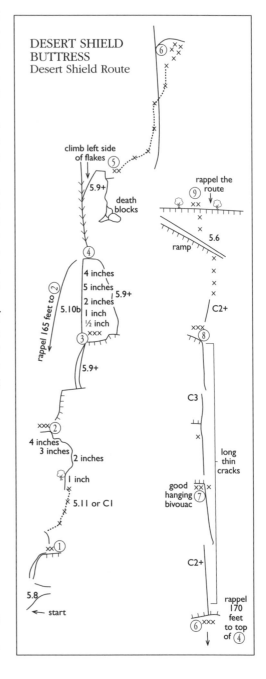

camming units; 3 sets of TCUs; 3 sets of stoppers

Approach: From the T intersection of Zion Canyon Road–Mount Carmel Highway, drive about 6 miles on Zion Canyon Road. Desert Shield Buttress is on the right. The route begins below and left of the main buttress.

Route: Pitch 1: Climb a right-angling ramp (jungle pitch) to a bolted belay on a ledge (5.8). Pitch 2: Move up and right, on the face above, past several bolts (5.11 or C1), to reach the base of a beautiful, widening and curving crack in black rock that leads to a bolted belay. Pitch 3: Move right and climb a left-facing corner/crack to a ledge, then a 5.9+ chimney that leads to a ledge with fixed anchors. Pitch 4: Climb the widening crack straight above the belay (it goes from ½ inch to 4 inches) to a belay on top of a flake (5.10). Pitch 5: Climb up a trough, then move right, on flakes that lead to the top of a pillar. Move right, to a fixed belay. Pitch 6: Work right, via bolts, to the crest of the corner of the buttress. Belay at fixed anchors. Pitches 7–8: Climb thin, beautiful cracks (C3) using sling belays. Pitch 9: Continue up the crack above the belay to a bolt ladder, then a 5.6 ramp to the left and then easy ground (bolt-protected) that leads to the top.

Special considerations: Leave ropes fixed between the top of pitch 4 and the top of pitch 6 for the return.

Descent: Rappel the route.

Climb 120, Desert Shield Buttress, Desert Shield. © Cameron M. Burns.

121 LEANING WALL, SPACE SHOT

First ascents: Ron Olevsky and Dave Jones, November 27–28, 1978. *First solo ascent:* Rich Strang, date unknown.

Difficulty: IV, 5.6, C1

Time: 1 full day

Equipment: 2 sets of camming units with extra hand-sized units; 2 sets of TCUs; 1 set of wired stoppers; 1 skyhook

Approach: From the T intersection of Zion Canyon Road–Mount Carmel

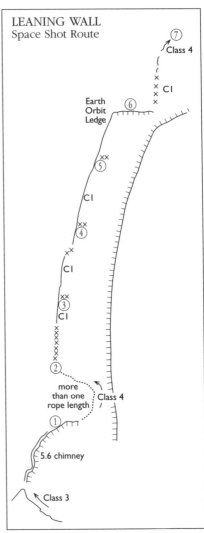

Climb 121, Leaning Wall, Space Shot. © Cameron M. Burns.

Highway, drive about 6.2 miles on Zion Canyon Road. Leaning Wall is on the right.

Route: Pitches 1–2: Climb (5.6) a chimney system on the left side of the large block sitting at the base of the Leaning Wall, which puts you at the start of the wall. Much of this section is loose and requires a little bit of routefinding. Pitch 3: Begin up the wall via a bolt ladder and thin crack (C1) to fixed anchors. Pitches 4–6: Follow the ever-widening crack system as it climbs up and right, across the Leaning Wall to the prominent Earth Orbit Ledge. Pitch 7: Move right, along Earth Orbit Ledge to a crack and bolt ladder system. Climb it (C1) to the top.

Special considerations: Beyond the anchors at the top of pitch 5, retreat is difficult due to the angle of the descent. Most of the belays are sling belays; a sling seat is recommended. In recent years a bolt at the top of pitch 7 came out and has not been replaced. A hook works well in the hole.

Descent: Scramble and down-climb far to the right (southeast) of the Leaning Wall, then make a series of rappels from fixed anchors on ledges.

122 TEMPLE OF SINAWAVA, MONKEYFINGER

First ascents: Ron Olevsky and Rob Schnelker, 1978. *First free ascent:* Mike O'Donnell and Craig Kenyon, 1989.
Difficulty: II, 5.9, C2 or 5.12a
Time: 1 full day
Equipment: 3 sets of camming units to #4, with extra hand-sized units; 2 sets of TCUs; stoppers
Approach: From the T intersection of Zion Canyon Road–Mount Carmel Highway, drive on Zion Canyon Road about 6.6 miles and find the parking area for Temple of Sinawava. The route climbs the obvious corner/crack system above the road.

Route: Pitch 1: Start by climbing an easy Class 5 pitch below and right of the route that leads to the base of the Pillar of Faith. Pitch 2: Climb the right side of the pillar to its top (5.10d or 5.9, C1). Pitch 3: Climb the Black Corner (5.12a or C1) to a 5.9 chimney. Pitch 4: Move right, around a roof (5.11 or C1), then up to a sling belay. Pitch 5: Continue up a 2-inch crack (5.10) to a belay. Pitch 6: Climb up to a C2 traverse out to the left (a variation climbs the 5.10a off-width above). The pitch ends at The Monkey House, a belay on a

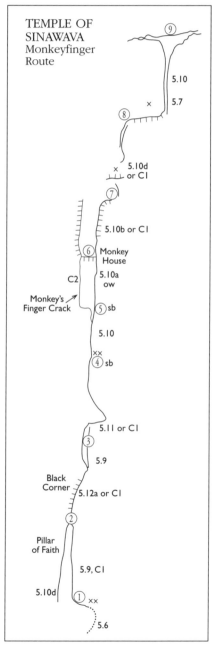

TEMPLE OF SINAWAVA
Monkeyfinger Route

⑨

5.10

⑧ × 5.7

× 5.10d
or C1

⑦

5.10b or C1

⑥ Monkey House

C2 5.10a ow

Monkey's Finger Crack ⑤ sb

5.10

xx
④ sb

5.11 or C1
③

5.9

Black Corner 5.12a or C1

②

Pillar of Faith

5.9, C1

5.10d ① xx

5.6

Climb 122, Temple of Sinawava, Monkeyfinger. © Cameron M. Burns.

ledge. Pitch 7: Climb the right side of the chimney above the Monkey House (5.10b or C1) to a decent ledge. Pitch 8: Move right, and climb a 5.10d or C1 crack/chimney to a ledge. Pitch 9: Move right, and climb a widening crack to the top.

Descent: Rappel the route.

123 THE PULPIT, ORIGINAL ROUTE

First ascent: Fred Beckey, Galen Rowell, Pat Callis, and Eric Bjørnstad, April 1967
Difficulty: I, 5.9
Time: 1 hour
Equipment: 1 set of camming units; 10 quickdraws
Approach: From the T intersection of Zion Canyon Road–Mount Carmel Highway, drive on Zion Canyon Road about 6.7 miles and find the parking area for The Pulpit.
Route: Climb a bolted face to a bolted crack, then to the summit.
Descent: Rappel from fixed anchors.

Climb 123, The Pulpit, Original Route. © Cameron M. Burns.

PINE CREEK CANYON

124 EAST TEMPLE, LOVELACE (A.K.A. FANG WALL)

First ascent: Dave Jones and Gary Gray, 1983
Difficulty: IV–V, 5.10, C2+
Time: 2 days
Equipment: 3 sets of camming units; off-width gear; a good selection of stoppers; 2 set of TCUs; Lowe Balls or equivalent

Approach: From the T intersection of Zion Canyon Road–Mount Carmel Highway, drive east on Mount Carmel Highway (Hwy. 9) for 0.5 mile to a small pullout on the left (north) side of the road just before a bridge. This is the best parking spot for routes on East Temple. This route climbs the beautiful red wall directly behind the Fang Spire, and follows a widening crack system to the canyon rim. To reach the first pitch, scramble up 220 feet of broken and bushy ledges to the base of the crack system.

Route: Pitch 1: Climb a long, right-facing corner to a prominent ledge (5.9). Pitch 2: Move right and climb the right side of a rounded flake (5.8). Pitch 3: Aid up a series of three very thin, side-by-side cracks (C2+) to gain a ledge on the left. Pitch 4: Climb the 5.9 right-facing corner above to a belay in a slot at the base of the white rock. Pitch 5: Continue straight up (5.9) to a stance. Pitch 6: There are two variations: The right one climbs wide, curving 5.10 cracks; the left one follows a crack that leads to 5.9 face-climbing. The pitch ends in a slot. Pitch 7: Climb the slot past

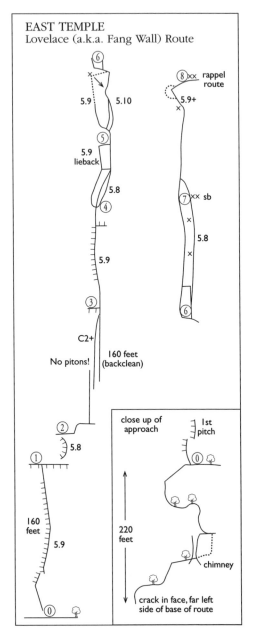

EAST TEMPLE
Lovelace (a.k.a. Fang Wall) Route

Climb 124, East Temple, Lovelace. © Cameron M. Burns.

bolts to a sling belay (5.8). Pitch 8: Continue up the crack, move left around an "ear," and gain a ledge with fixed anchors (5.9+).

Special considerations: The route goes entirely clean, including pitch 3. As with all Zion routes, many parties use points of clean aid here and there.

Descent: Rappel the route.

125 EAST TEMPLE, FANG SPIRE

First ascent: Kyle Copeland and John Middendorf, 1988
Difficulty: IV–V, 5.9, C3
Time: 2 days

Climb 125, East Temple, Fang Spire. © Cameron M. Burns.

Equipment: 3 sets of TCUs; 2 sets of camming units; 2 sets of stoppers; RPs

Approach: From the ⊤ intersection of Zion Canyon Road–Mount Carmel Highway, drive east up Mount Carmel Highway (Hwy. 9) for 0.5 mile to a small pullout on the left (north) side of the road just before a bridge; park here. The route starts on the left side of the base of the tower's southeast face, up a curving (to the left) crack.

Route: Pitch 1: Climb the curving crack, which leads to a huge ledge and fixed anchors (5.9, C1). Pitch 2: Walk to the right, jump down to a ledge, then move right, into a chimney (5.9 or C1). Climb it and exit it to the left, following thin features to a ledge with fixed anchors (C2+). Pitch 3: Climb a 4-inch crack above the ledge, which leads to a 5.9+ crack, then a bolt traverse right and a short crack ending at a ledge (5.9, C3). Pitch 4: Move up and right, on bolts and hooks (C0). Pitch 5:

Climb the right side of a funky flake using hooks, rivets, and bolts, over two roofs to a sling belay. Pitch 6: Continue hooking and using bolts/rivets to a ledge. Mantle it and move left, then climb the left side of the tower to a fixed belay (5.7, C3). Pitch 7: Scramble to the top.

Special considerations: The route goes entirely clean now, but take a good supply of hooks.

Descent: Rappel the route.

126 EAST TEMPLE, COWBOY BOB GOES TO ZION

First ascent: Hugh O'Neill and Dave Jones, 1986
Difficulty: IV–V, 5.10+, C2
Time: 1–2 days
Equipment: 3 sets of camming units to #5 Camalot; 1 set of TCUs; stoppers

Approach: From the T intersection of Zion Canyon Road–Mount Carmel Highway, drive east up Mount Carmel Highway (Hwy. 9) for 0.5 mile to a small pullout on the left (north) side of the road just before a bridge; park here. On the south face of East Temple are three prominent, pointed subsidiary summits—the Towers of the Three Fates. Cowboy Bob climbs the right side of the leftmost tower. The route begins 100 feet below the highest scree field at the top of a slab, 50 feet below a Class 3 gully leading up and left from the top of the scree slope.

Route: Pitch 1: Climb the obvious vertical hand crack above the slab for a full rope length to a belay on a protrusion (5.10+). Pitch 2: Continue up the crack (5.9) to a ledge system. Move the

EAST TEMPLE, FANG SPIRE

belay to the right end of the ledge system. Pitch 3: Cross the Class 3 gully (mentioned in the Approach) and climb a concave face up and left to a belay at a ledge. Pitch 4: Move back right (not the crack up and left of the belay), to gain a shallow, eroded

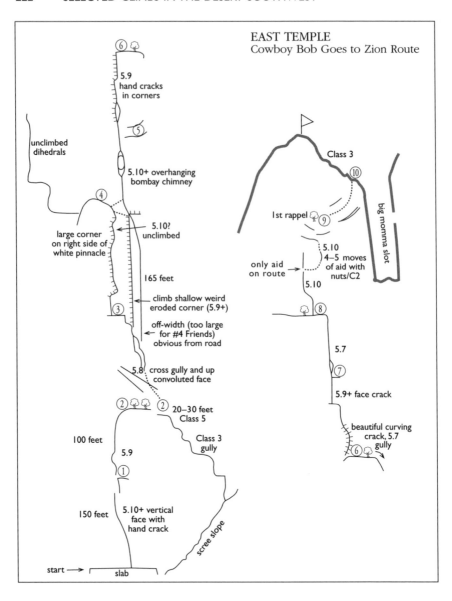

EAST TEMPLE
Cowboy Bob Goes to Zion Route

6

5.9
hand cracks
in corners

5

unclimbed
dihedrals

5.10+ overhanging
bombay chimney

4

Class 3

10

1st rappel 9

big momma slot

large corner
on right side of
white pinnacle

5.10?
unclimbed

5.10
4–5 moves
of aid with
nuts/C2

only aid
on route

5.10

165 feet

climb shallow weird
eroded corner (5.9+)

3

8

off-width (too large
for #4 Friends)
obvious from road

5.7

5.8 cross gully and up
convoluted face

7

5.9+ face crack

2   2   20–30 feet
Class 5

100 feet

Class 3
gully

5.9

beautiful curving
crack, 5.7
gully

6

1

150 feet

5.10+ vertical
face with
hand crack

scree slope

start →   slab

corner (don't climb the off-width to the right of that); climb it for a full rope length to a roof, then move left to a belay atop a pillar (5.9). Pitches 5–6: From the 4th belay, move right, to join the crack leading to a bombay chimney, and continue up right-facing corners to reach a big ledge (5.10+). Pitch 7: Move left and climb a nice, curving crack (5.7) to a crack in the face (5.9+) leading to a stance. Pitch 8: Climb the crack/corner above to a ledge (5.7). Pitch 9: Climb a 5.10 crack above the belay, move to the right on clean aid, then climb an unprotected 5.10 slab/face above. Pitch 10: Work up and right, to the ridge, then scramble to the top.

Climb 126, East Temple, Cowboy Bob Goes to Zion. © Cameron M. Burns.

Special considerations: The route goes entirely clean and has only four or five aid moves. There are no rappel anchors on the route.

Descent: From the top of the route, make two rappels down the ridge to the right (east), then four more rappels down a gully to the top of the scree slope.

127 EAST TEMPLE, UNCERTAIN FATES
First ascent: Stacy Allison and Dave Jones, 1986
Difficulty: IV–V, 5.11a, C1 or 5.11+
Time: 1–2 days
Equipment: 3 sets of camming units to #5; 1 set of TCUs; stoppers

Approach: From the T intersection of Zion Canyon Road–Mount Carmel Highway, drive east up Mount Carmel Highway (Hwy. 9) for 0.5 mile to a small pullout on the left (north) side of the road just before a bridge; park here. On the south face of East Temple are three prominent, pointed subsidiary summits—the Towers of the Three Fates. This route climbs the right side of the middle tower. Scramble up to a large, bushy ledge below the middle tower. The route starts up a crack in a deep recess in the wall above the ledge.

Route: Pitch 1: Climb the left of two cracks in a deep recessed slot to a belay (5.9). Pitch 2: Continue straight up an off-width for a full rope length (5.10+). Pitch 3: Climb a right-facing corner, then move right, around the prow of the arête, and continue up to a belay ledge (5.9). Pitch 4: Climb a stunning face crack (5.9) to a thinner crack (5.11+ or C1), then climb over a roof to a right-facing corner (5.10d)

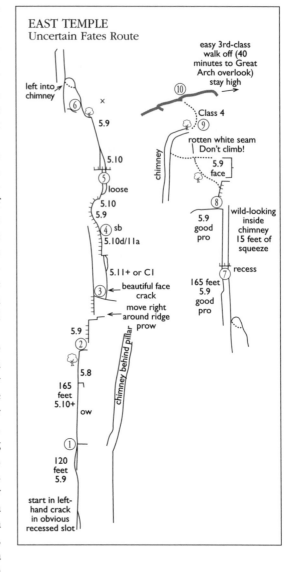

that leads to a sling belay. Pitch 5: Climb the right side of a curving flake/corner around a roof, then up loose rock to a belay (5.10). Pitch 6: Climb over a roof, then continue up left-trending cracks to a belay (5.10). Pitch 7: Move left into a chimney, then climb it for a full rope length to a belay (5.9). Pitch 8: Chimney straight up (5.9), then move left to a belay ledge. Pitch 9: Climb a short left-facing corner, then move left onto 5.9 face-climbing to the base of a rotten white seam. (Don't climb the seam.) Move left into a chimney. Climb the chimney to a belay at its top. Pitch 10: Climb Class 4 to the top.

Descent: Walk off to the right (east) and back to Mount Carmel Highway.

Climb 127, East Temple, Uncertain Fates. © Cameron M. Burns.

128 ASHTAR COMMAND, NORTH FACE

First ascent: Unknown
Difficulty: II, 5.9
Time: 1 hour
Equipment: 1 set of camming units with extra hand-sized units; 10
quickdraws

Approach: From the T intersection of Zion Canyon Road–Mount Carmel
Highway, drive east up the Mount Carmel Highway (Hwy. 9) about 3.5 miles until
the last switchback and the start of the Tunnels. Roughly 0.1 mile before the en-

Climb 128, Ashtar Command, North Face. © Cameron M. Burns.

trance of the first tunnel is a small yellow sign; on the slope above this sign, about 70 feet from the road, is the small leaning tower of Ashtar Command. The standard route on the tower (the two-pitch North Face route) faces the road.

Route: Pitch 1: Climb a 5.8 hand/finger crack to fixed anchors. Pitch 2: Climb a bolted 5.9 face to the summit.

Special considerations: This route probably gets more traffic than any other route in Zion National Park during the summer. Be on your best behavior and don't park where it'll annoy the rangers. Also, the area is often closed in the spring for nesting peregrine falcons. Check at the visitor center before climbing.

Descent: Rappel the route.

129 TUNNELS AREA, THE HEADACHE

First ascent: Brian Smith and Dana Geary, August 1975
Difficulty: II–III, 5.10
Time: ½ day
Equipment: Several sets of camming units, with extra medium (hand and fist) sizes

Approach: On the Mount Carmel Highway near the tunnels, park along the north side of the road, then hike toward the first tunnel. Do not enter the tunnel, however; walk around its outside for 50 feet and The Headache, a stunning, obvious, three-pitch hand crack, becomes obvious above the trail.

Route: Pitch 1: Climb 5.9 hands and fingers over a small roof to a bolted belay. Pitch 2: Climb 5.9 hands to a bolted belay. Pitch 3: Continue up the widening crack to the top (5.10).

Climb 129, Tunnels Area, The Headache. © Cameron M. Burns.

Special considerations: The area is often closed in the spring for nesting peregrine falcons. Check at the visitor center before climbing.

Descent: Rappel the wide crack that sits immediately left of the route.

130 TUNNELS AREA, MASTERBLASTER
First ascent: Ron Olevsky and McLaughlin, June 1986
Difficulty: II, 5.5, C1
Time: 3 hours
Equipment: 5 sets of Friends from #1 to #2; 1 #2.5 to #4 Friends; 2 sets of TCUs; large stoppers

Tunnels Area: climb 130, Masterblaster; climb 129, The Headache.
© Cameron M. Burns.

Approach: On Mount Carmel Highway near the tunnels, park along the north side of the road, then hike toward the first tunnel. Do not enter the tunnel, however; walk around its outside for 50 feet and continue up the hill east to a low-angled gully system, about 160 feet past (left of) The Headache (climb 129). Masterblaster takes the obvious splitter crack through the steep roof on the left side of the gully, about 150 feet above the bottom of the gully. Scramble up the low-angled gully (Class 4–lower Class 5) to the base of the splitter crack.

Route: Pitch 1: Climb the crack out the roof (C1) to anchors just above the lip of the roof. Pitch 2: Continue up the crack to a second set of anchors (C1).

Special considerations: Many parties do only the first pitch. The area is often closed in the spring for nesting peregrine falcons. Check at the visitor center before climbing.

Descent: Make one double-rope rappel from the top of the route.

LOWER CANYON

131 THREE MARYS, GENTLEMAN'S AGREEMENT

First ascent: Ron Olevsky and Scott Fischer, April 1982
Difficulty: IV, 5.9, C2
Time: 1–2 days
Equipment: 3 sets of camming units; 3 sets of TCUs; 2 sets of stoppers; bolt kit and rappel slings for descent

Climb 131, Three Marys, Gentleman's Agreement. ©Cameron M. Burns.

Approach: From the locked gate at the end of the road leading to the "Dixie College: Obert C. Tanner Amphitheater," about 0.7 mile from Hwy. 9, walk west up the paved road until the Three Marys are obvious ahead and right. Hike up to the southeast side (bottom right) of the leftmost (southwesternmost) Mary. The hike takes at least an hour. Gentleman's Agreement climbs the obvious huge dihedral splitting the formation's southeast corner.

Route: Pitch 1: Climb loose blocks 20 feet (5.8), clip a bolt, and swing into the right-facing corner on aid. (There's an old drilled hook hole here.) Clean aid on

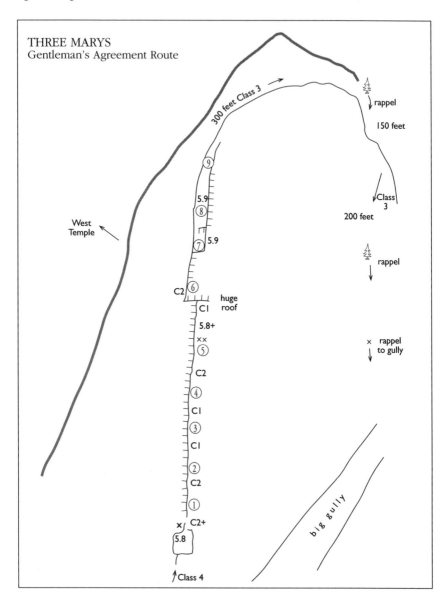

THREE MARYS
Gentleman's Agreement Route

300 feet Class 3

rappel

150 feet

⑨

5.9

⑧

West Temple

⑦ 5.9

Class 3

200 feet

rappel

C2 ⑥

huge

C1 roof

5.8+

xx

⑤

rappel to gully

C2

④

C1

③

C1

②

C2

①

x C2+

5.8

big gully

↑ Class 4

steep rock (C2+) leads to a sling belay. Pitches 2–4: Continue on clean aid up the crack as it progressively widens, using natural gear for belays (C2). Pitch 5: Continue on clean aid to a bolt belay. Pitch 6: Lay-back (5.8+) to a 15-foot roof, then aid straight out the roof on #4 Camalots to a finger-sized corner. Continue up the corner to a ledge (C2). Pitch 7: Chimney (5.9) to a ledge. Pitch 8: Continue up the crack system (5.9, C1). Pitch 9: Free-climb (5.9) to a tree at the top of the cliff. Then scramble for 300 feet up slabs to the high point of the Third Mary.

Special considerations: There are no fixed anchors at any of the belays, except the belay at the top of pitch 5. Belays are where you make them. The route goes all clean, but needs a bolt on the first pitch between the existing bolt and the start of the corner. For the descent, the existing anchors, which are few, are difficult to locate. Also, several attempts by strong climbers to free-climb this route have failed.

Descent: Scramble to the northeast side of the formation and locate slings on a pine tree. Rappel 150 feet. Then downclimb 200 feet of Class 3, heading toward the gully separating the southwest Mary from the center Mary, to another tree with a rappel sling. Make two double-rope rappels from anchors into the gully between the two Marys. Scramble down the gully 400 feet or until it is necessary to make a 40-foot rappel to the ground from a fixed anchor.

132 MOUNT KINESAVA, KING CORNER

First ascent: Mike Baker and Bob Wade, March 1994
Difficulty: V, 5.10, A3
Time: 1–2 days
Equipment: 3 sets of TCUs; 3 sets of Camalots to #5; 2 sets of stoppers; a dozen small pitons, from Birdbeaks to ½-inch angles
Approach: From the parking lot for the Chinle Trail in the Anasazi Plateau

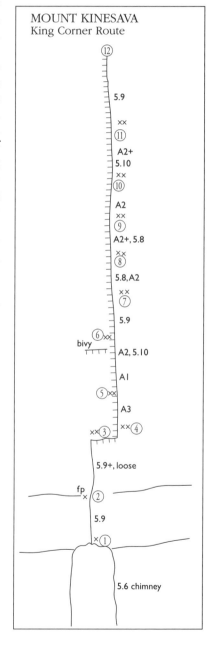

MOUNT KINESAVA
King Corner Route

Mt. Kinesava's south face, Zion National Park. King Corner follows the huge dihedral in the center of the photo that begins at the sun/shadow line. © Cameron M. Burns.

subdivision, follow the Chinle Trail for about 3 miles to the base of the south face of Mount Kinesava. The route begins directly below the huge corner on the south face of Mount Kinesava.

Route: Pitch 1: Climb a 5.6 chimney to a ledge with fixed anchors. Pitch 2: Climb a crack above the ledge to a fixed piton (5.9). Pitch 3: Continue straight up loose rock to a large ledge with fixed anchors (good bivy site). Pitch 4: Move right, to the base of the King Corner, and belay at fixed anchors. Pitches 5–12: Climb the corner. There is a decent bivy hole inside the chimney on pitch 6.

Special considerations: This route will likely go clean.

Descent: The descent is tricky. From the top of the route, climb up over a ridge, then down-climb (with one rappel) to a large meadow on the east side of Mount Kinesava. With the addition of anchors below the corner itself, the route could be rappelled easily.

ANNOTATED BIBLIOGRAPHY

Bjørnstad, Eric. *Desert Rock.* Evergreen, Colo.: Chockstone Press, 1988. Out of print. The classic reference on desert climbing.

———. *Desert Rock I: Rock Climbs in the National Parks.* Evergreen, Colo.: Chockstone Press, 1994. Part of Bjørnstad's new series on desert rock climbing. Covers a selection of routes in the Southwest's national parks.

———. *Desert Rock II: Wall Street to San Rafael Swell.* Evergreen, Colo.: Chockstone Press, 1996. Covers the San Rafael Swell, Wall Street, and various other areas east of the Colorado River.

———. *Rock Climbing Desert Rock III: Moab to Colorado National Monument.* Evergreen, Colo.: Chockstone Press, 1999.

Copeland, Kyle. *A Climber's Guide to Wall Street.* Moab, Utah: Self-published, 1989. The first guide to climbing along Wall Street. Now there are at least four more guides covering Wall Street.

Green, Stewart. *Rock Climbing Utah.* Helena, Mont.: Falcon Press, 1998. Covers selected climbing areas throughout Utah, including many desert areas.

Knapp, Fred. *Classic Desert Climbs.* Boulder, Colo.: Sharp End Publishing, 1995. Covers a smattering of routes from throughout the most popular desert areas.

McMullen, John. *Quick Clips: 120 Tips to Improve Your Technique, Performance and Equipment.* Carbondale, Colo.: Elk Mountain Press, 1997. This little book published by *Climbing Magazine* has a number of excellent tips on wall- and aid-climbing techniques that can be useful in the desert.

Middendorf, John, and John Long. *Big Walls.* Evergreen, Colo.: Chockstone Press, 1994. An excellent reference for wall- and aid-climbing neophytes.

INDEX

Names of routes are set in italics.

ABOUT THE AUTHOR

Australian-born Cameron M. Burns is a Colorado-based writer and climber. He has authored hundreds of magazine and newspaper articles about rock, ice, and mountain climbing, and written five climbing guidebooks, including *Colorado Ice Climber's Guide* and *Climbing California's Fourteeners*. He lives in Basalt, Colorado, with his wife, Ann, his dog, Lefty, and two cats, Nicholas and Morrigan.

Cameron M. Burns on Standing Rock, after his third trip up the spire. Photo: Jon Butler/Burns collection.

ABOUT THE MOUNTAINEERS

THE MOUNTAINEERS, founded in 1906, is a nonprofit outdoor activity and conservation club, whose mission is "to explore, study, preserve, and enjoy the natural beauty of the outdoors. . . ." Based in Seattle, Washington, the club is now the third-largest such organization in the United States, with 15,000 members and five branches throughout Washington State.

The Mountaineers sponsors both classes and year-round outdoor activities in the Pacific Northwest, which include hiking, mountain climbing, ski-touring, snowshoeing, bicycling, camping, kayaking and canoeing, nature study, sailing, and adventure travel. The club's conservation division supports environmental causes through educational activities, sponsoring legislation, and presenting informational programs. All club activities are led by skilled, experienced volunteers, who are dedicated to promoting safe and responsible enjoyment and preservation of the outdoors.

If you would like to participate in these organized outdoor activities or the club's programs, consider a membership in The Mountaineers. For information and an application, write or call The Mountaineers, Club Headquarters, 300 Third Avenue West, Seattle, Washington 98119; (206) 284-6310.

The Mountaineers Books, an active, nonprofit publishing program of the club, produces guidebooks, instructional texts, historical works, natural history guides, and works on environmental conservation. All books produced by The Mountaineers are aimed at fulfilling the club's mission.

Send or call for our catalog of more than 300 outdoor titles:

The Mountaineers Books
1001 SW Klickitat Way, Suite 201
Seattle, WA 98134
800-553-4453
mbooks@mountaineers.org
www.mountaineersbooks.org